CHILDREN
OF
POVERTY

Studies on the Effects of Single Parenthood, the Feminization of Poverty, and Homelessness

edited by

STUART BRUCHEY
University of Maine

A GARLAND SERIES

SIDEWALKS TALK

A Naturalistic Study of Street Kids

KATHERINE COLEMAN LUNDY

GARLAND PUBLISHING, Inc.
New York & London / 1995

Library of Congress Cataloging-in-Publication Data

Lundy, Katherine Coleman, 1952–
    Sidewalks talk : a naturalistic study of street kids / Katherine
Coleman Lundy.
        p.   cm.
    Includes bibliographical references and index.
    ISBN 0-8153-2014-0 (alk. paper)
    1. Street children—United States—Case studies.   2. Homeless
youth—United States—Case studies.   I. Title.
HV881.L85   1995
362.7'6'0973—dc20   94-42201
                                                                              CIP

Printed on acid-free, 250-year-life paper
Manufactured in the United States of America

to M. E. R.

1914 – 1994

The streets are terrible, you know. Sidewalks talk and you'd better watch what you do and what you say. I mean, sidewalks talk, that means everybody's out to get you. You've got to know who to trust and who not to trust. 'Cause sidewalks talk . . .

Sarah

Contents

Acknowledgements

A number of individuals contributed to the evolution and completion of this manuscript, whose influence I acknowledge here. The interest and investment my informants brought to the research is gratefully acknowledged. My life is the richer for knowing each of them and the many other youths I was privileged to know in my years at *The One*.

I am indebted to my parents, J. Paul Coleman and Jane Rogers Coleman, whose moral and material support of this effort were vital to its completion. My aunt, Martha E. Rogers, provided a commanding example of nursing scholarship, and on occasion, food, shelter, and child care. My siblings, John P. Coleman and Marti Coleman, sustained my sense of family and connectedness during my years of doctoral study. My daughter, Lara Elisabeth Lundy, remained companionable, warm, and encouraging through long months of my preoccupation and inattention.

My committee, John Phillips, Margot Ely, and Judith Lothian, were wholehearted in their support of my research and generous with direction, guidance, and instruction. John was calm and encouraging, meticulous in his attention to detail, and Judy expressed her confidence in my vision and its ultimate worth. Margot, an astute and incisive scholar, brought wisdom, experience, and focus to my own research.

My peer support group members, Michael Boyle and Dorit Amir, were valued for their insight and encouragement. Madeleine Unger has been and remains a constant and sustaining presence. A relative newcomer to my circle, Kelly

Mayo has supported me with her presence, friendship, and counsel.

Colleagues at the crisis center were most supportive of my work—Olga Hernandez and Deborah Lynch in administration, Cynthia Lipman, Neil Margetson, and Chris Bohling of the research department, and Micheline in outreach were quick to facilitate my research endeavor, permitting me to work with the outreach program, Off the Streets. Outreach staff, Terry, Melvin, Coddington, and Claude, initially chary of me as an outsider, received me graciously into their company upon evidence of my commitment to the kids. Gifted counselors, these four embodied compassion, tenderness, and affirmation toward street youths even as they confronted the youths about their lives. Greg Loken of Legal Services and Pat in Support Services provided valuable assistance with document retrieval.

I was privileged to have as my mentor and friend Dr. James T. Kennedy, then Medical Director. He emboldened me to risk working with street kids and supported me fully in this position. His commitment, and that of other Health Services staff, to "do the right thing," effected a milieu that saw state of the art health care made available to this vulnerable population.

With my own family at some distance, Judith and James Lothian and their family assumed a prominent position in my life, embracing me and my child as their own. Colleagues and friends Ann Greene, Therese Meehan, Nancy Oliver, Ann Morgan, Judy Urban, Maria Prieto, Deirdre Bastible, and Eileen Barrett provided support and encouragement throughout the research process.

Many friends not connected with school or work enriched my journey—Steve Raborn, Jeanne Howe, Heidi Hayter Sanchez, Cynthia Bournazos, Barbara Schwerin, John and Ellen Clarkson, Victoria Bailey, Emily Tatum, Darryl Green, and

Carlos Alomar possess a special place in my affections, notwithstanding time and distance. We had our fun!

Several individuals were forthcoming with assistance as I worked to confirm and procure obscure materials. My sister, Marti Coleman; Colonel J.L. Maynard of The Citadel; James Converso of the *New York Post*; Kate Scott Douglas at MCA; research staff at Columbia and Sire Records; reference librarians at the New York and Charleston County Public Libraries; and employees of Rounds in New York, Pic-a-Flick Video, Sensations Records and Tapes, and the Record Bar in Charleston were critical to the success of this endeavor.

Finally, I wish to thank Kim Jones for her patient labor in transcribing informant interviews and George M. Campbell, computer hack and manuscript editor nonpareil, for his meticulous preparation of this manuscript.

That these influences converged in time and place to enable my completion of this volume is, I believe, providential. The lines have fallen in pleasant places.

Sidewalks Talk

I

The Problem and
Research Question

In the early weeks and months of my employment as a
nurse clinician at a crisis center for runaway and homeless
teenagers, I encountered an occasional youth whose alienation
from society was extraordinary and profound. I speak of them
by name, but for this document, all names and identifying
characteristics have been changed. Sarah, a wraith-like
Dominican girl of fourteen, had been on the streets
intermittently since she was nine, surviving by stealing, dealing,
and prostitution. Bo, a tall lanky blond youth of eighteen,
possessed of a raffish charm, was a hustler and drug user of
prodigious proportions. Recently, I have seen Bo sleeping in a
park, hustling food stamps, scavenging through garbage cans for
food, and wandering barefoot in winter. Sarah and Bo have kept
in touch with me over the years. Sarah turned nineteen this Fall
on the streets, having failed multiple attempts at rehabilitation.
Bo was last seen shuffling down Second Avenue, unbathed,
unkempt, blanketed and muttering.

Mandy and Benjamin are two youths I have seen only once.
Mandy, a tall lissome girl with dark hair and pale skin, had lost
custody of her daughter and now wandered the streets alone,
seeking shelter in abandoned buildings. I treated her for
sexually transmitted diseases, commenting that she must have
a lot of pain to use such an array of mind numbing substances.
Her tears confirmed my perceptions. I thought I had made a
connection with her, but she did not return. Benjamin came to

me on his seventeenth birthday. An uncle had sought him out in the inner recesses of Penn Station and was to take him out to celebrate. I treated Ben's extreme lice infestation, gave him clothes and a shower, and wished him a Happy Birthday. After he left, I reflected on what his life must be like in the station's underground labyrinth—the searing heat of summer, the aching cold of winter, and incomprehensible bleakness throughout.

My interest in street kids was piqued by these experiences and by articles in various lay publications that described street kids as existing in a nether world of drugs, prostitution, violence, and isolation. I came to consider that an informed awareness of street life might facilitate my work with these youths.

Of the one million or so youths who leave home every year, as many as 50,000 are absent for more than a year (Office of the Inspector General, 1983). Runaways from healthier families tend to return home (Kennedy et al., 1990; V. Price, 1989), but youths from less functional families may run repeatedly, and eventually not return (Saltonstall, 1984). Many youths never return home (Opinion Research Corporation, 1976). The more fortunate of these young people are able to establish self-sufficiency within the community (Hartman, Burgess, & McCormack, 1987). The less fortunate, exhausting available community supports such as friends and relatives (Shaffer & Caton, 1984), are soon compelled to the streets (Citizen's Committee for Children of New York, 1983; Office of the Inspector General, 1983; V. Price, 1989; Saltonstall, 1984). Conservative estimates place the number of youths "on the streets" at 250,000 to 1,000,000 nationwide (Office of the Inspector General, 1983; J.M. Robertson, 1988), although "no empirical basis for a national estimate exists" (M.J. Robertson, 1989, p. 5).

"The street," according to Hartman et al. (1987), is "an open environment that is unprotective, enticing, and exploitative" (p. 294). The street youth is defined by Ritter (1989) as a young person "who has separated himself from his family, has abandoned any pretense that he has a family, and now relates almost entirely to the street" (p. 157). Wilkinson (1987)[1] defines a street kid as a youth as young as 10 or 11, and as old as 22, who spends most of his waking hours in areas frequented by other street kids and who engages in street activities, whether or not the youth is actually homeless. Her definition extends to youths who maintain apartments and accommodate other street kids. C. Williams (1993) cites the Inter-NGO definition of a street child as being

> any boy or girl who has not reached adulthood for whom the street (in the widest sense of the word, including unoccupied dwellings, wasteland, etc.) has become her or his habitual abode and sources of livelihood and who is inadequately protected, supervised or directed by responsible adults. (p. 832)

I have used the definition as articulated by Wilkinson (1987) in this study. Street kids have been designated by many names (Kennedy et al., 1990), but I have used the terms street kids and street youths interchangeably to refer to this population.

Despite greater awareness of homelessness generally, the homeless adolescent population remains a nearly invisible subculture (J.M. Robertson, 1988). Estranged and alienated from family and other supportive structures, these youths congregate in isolated areas and seek to avoid contact with mainstream institutions and individuals (Caton, 1986; Deisher & Farrow, 1986; Kennedy et al., 1990; Manov & Lowther, 1983; Wilkinson, 1987).

Anecdotal and empirical evidence suggests that street youths are likely to have run from or been thrown out of extremely disordered homes (Adams, Gullotta, & Clancy, 1985; Citizens' Committee, 1983; Crystal, 1986; Office of the Inspector General, 1983; V. Price, 1989; Saltonstall, 1984). Multiple sources document the presence of intense family conflicts that are often manifested in physical, sexual, or psychological abuse (Farber, Kinast, McCoard, & Falkner, 1984; Janus, Burgess, & McCormack, 1987; Saltonstall, 1984; Stiffman, 1989). Family disruption, substance abuse by parental figures, introduction of transient parental consorts, and role reversal often contribute further to a sense of instability, unpredictability, and chaos within the home (Mirkin, Raskin, & Antognini, 1984; V. Price, 1989; Roberts, 1982a, 1982b; Saltonstall, 1984). Notably, a substantial number of street youths have been discharged or have run from foster care or other institutional placement (Citizens' Committee, 1983; Hartman et al., 1987; Shaffer & Caton, 1984; Wilkinson, 1987).

Emotional impoverishment and poor self-esteem have been correlated with runaway behavior (Beyer, 1974; Englander, 1984; Powers, Jaklitsch, & Eckenrode, 1988; V. Price, 1989; Roberts, 1982a; A. Williams, 1977). Maladaptive coping behaviors (Roberts, 1982a) and a diminished sense of mastery of the environment (V. Price, 1989) have also been noted. Runaway youths commonly evince poor school performance, marginal social acceptance, and drug use prior to the acute separation (Crystal, 1986; V. Price, 1989; Roberts, 1982a, 1982b).

Upon separation from the family, the exigencies of survival on the streets are often rapidly felt. Many youths learn to exchange their bodies for a place to stay, and others may turn to prostitution, stealing, drug-dealing, or panhandling (Wilkinson, 1987). Abuse, victimization, violent and traumatic injury, substance abuse, and illness related to exposure and inadequate hygiene are commonly encountered (Kennedy et al., 1990; Yates, MacKenzie, Pennbridge, & Cohen, 1988).

The family dynamics, personality attributes, and consequences associated with runaway and nomadic lifestyles have been documented at length (Stiffman, 1989). Life on the streets is agreed to "erode the emotional and physical welfare of the abandoned child" (Kennedy et al., 1990, p. 87)[2]. However, few studies have described in detailed and concrete terms the experiences of kids on the streets from their own vantage point (Caton, 1986; Institute of Medicine, 1988; Kaplan, 1989; McCarthy & Hagan, 1992; M.J. Robertson, 1989).

The present study is an attempt to redress the paucity of information about street youths' daily lives, experiences, and perceptions by describing in detail segments of the lives and experiences of a small group of street kids—to see the world through their eyes, and to identify patterns in the commonalities and varieties of their experiences. Through the center where I worked I studied a small group of street youths to generate first-hand knowledge of these adolescents' experiences, priorities, and concerns. The information provided by this study is meant to contribute richly documented pictures of this small group of street kids that may enhance health professionals' awareness and understanding of this vulnerable population.

The research question was, "What are the lived experiences of a small group of street youths?" Subquestions that evolved about this group over the course of the study were:

1. What are the social contacts of this small group of street youths? What is the "group life" of these youths on the street?

2. What survival strategies do these youths use in coping on the streets?

3. What tacit knowledge enables them to survive?

4. What are the relationships of these street youths to mainstream society?

5. What qualities, attitudes, and values do they manifest?

Notes

1. Similarly in Covenant House New Jersey, 1990a and 1990b.
2. Similarly in J.M. Robertson, 1988.

II

Review of the Literature

Introduction

I have attempted in the preceding chapter to establish that a discrete population of estranged youths exists whose lives unfold in the scant refuge of the streets. Their numbers are substantial; with estimates consistently ranging at or in excess of 250,000 (Office of the Inspector General, 1983). They are essentially homeless and familyless (Kennedy et al., 1990; Ritter, 1989), having fled from or been rejected by extremely disordered families. The antecedents and consequences of such flight have been well defined. Lacking was a detailed elaboration of the day-to-day aspects of life on the streets for youths so engaged, that I, by means of this study, have sought to provide.

Qualitative research differs from quantitative research in that the relevant literature emerges as data analysis progresses. Discussion of studies salient to my findings is presented in subsequent chapters. In the present chapter I review extant qualitative research pertaining to runaway and street kids and consider current thought with respect to the dynamics that compel street kids to remain on the streets. This literature, though sparse, is of particular relevance to my research as it presents attempts to describe and interpret the experiences of street youths.

Runaway and Street Kids

Wilkinson (1987) conducted a seminal study of street kids in Spokane, Washington, collecting data through observation and interview. In Spokane, a preponderance of street youths maintained nominal connections with their families of origin and evinced a street lifestyle primarily during the warmer seasons. Wilkinson identified street kids as being of four types—female prostitutes, male prostitutes, *punk rockers*, and *stoners*. Noting that the four groups rarely intermingled, she investigated only the two latter groups, punk rockers and stoners. The four groups were distinguished by their clothing, the areas frequented, and means of support. Commonalities among the two latter groups included dependence on drugs and a proclivity for "partying," or "getting drunk, getting stoned" with other street kids (p. 107).

Wilkinson (1987) indicated that her respondents left home secondary to family conflict and entered street life through friends and acquaintances involved in the street lifestyle. Prostitution, panhandling, drug dealing, and scamming were identified as survival strategies street youths were seen to employ. Various living arrangements observed by Wilkinson were staying with friends in independently held apartments, with friends' families, their own families or relatives, or entering a sexual relationship in exchange for domicile. Her informants also pooled funds to share a room or apartment, or, as a last resort, slept outdoors in parks, under bridges, or in other semiprotected areas.

In this formative study of street kids, Wilkinson (1987) elaborated basic patterns of life practiced by street kids; however, her study does not convey the thick rich descriptions of street youths and their subjective experiences essential to a deeper understanding of these youths. Further, she limited her informants to two of the four types she identified. My research differed from Wilkinson's in two important ways—my own research evolved to complement Wilkinson's, in that I focused on female prostitutes, male hustlers, and male transvestite prostitutes; and Wilkinson conducted her research at a time when AIDS and crack were relatively obscure—phenomena of considerable import to my sample.

McCarthy of McCarthy and Hagan (1992) conducted an intensive descriptive survey of street kids in Canada. The authors indicated that street life was characterized by a relentless search—for shelter, food, work, school, social assistance, and friendship. Their work described these activities in considerable detail, together with a discussion of criminal activities and affective states of their informants. They concluded that "combining field studies, interviews, and self-report questionnaires in one research project would provide more extensive data on homeless youth" (p. 429) than the present study.

Sereny (1985) conducted intensive interviews with young female prostitutes in North America, West Germany, and Great Britain during the late seventies and early eighties. Her informants worked exclusively with pimps, who if somewhat abusive, provided a measure of support and structure, along with food, clothing and shelter. Sereny acknowledged that her informants had experienced neglect and family conflict, but she denied indications of the extreme family dysfunction and chaos observed in later studies.

Weisberg's (1985) descriptive ethnography encompassed adolescent straight, gay, and transvestite male prostitutes and female prostitutes. Most, if not all, were consistently domiciled, renting or sharing hotel rooms or flats with other youths, or living for varying periods with dates or lovers. Weisberg indicated that adolescent prostitution assumed different forms. Youths engaging in situational prostitution did so infrequently, to supplement other income or allowances. Gay and transvestite prostitutes were more likely to engage in habitual, or frequent prostitution, bringing to their vocation reasoned qualities of ambition, intent, service, and organization. Such youths also derived a sense of identity and an outlet for their sexuality through the social interactions with the gay community prostitution provided. Straight male prostitutes, in contrast, moved among the peer-delinquent subculture pursuing prostitution, drug dealing, panhandling, and petty criminal activity indiscriminately. One informant summarized the attitudes these youths espoused: "remember, all of life is a hustle" (p. 28).

While Sereny (1985) made little mention of drug use among her informants, Weisberg (1985) reported the frequent use of alcohol, amphetamines, and hallucinogens by her subjects.

Aptekar (1988) reported on his study of Colombian street children in *The street children of Cali*. With a team of university graduate students, Aptekar "spent time with the children as they ate, played, worked, and even slept, so that we could share the variety of experiences they had as they moved around the city" (p. xv). Following the children through the streets, a social service agency, and the state juvenile detention center, the researchers collected data through observation, interviews, and a battery of psychological tests.

Aptekar (1988) argued that street children existed in Colombian society as a consequence of extreme poverty and the social upheaval which followed Colombia's struggle for independence. This upheaval saw the conservative values of the ruling Spanish patriarchy severely threatened by the opposing values of an African matriarchy and the independent children the latter spawned, with the result that the government sought to contain "by action and remedy" (p. 45) the children's "wayward lifestyles."

Aptekar (1988) elaborated a two-level typology of street children. Prepubescent youths, aged six to twelve, were of two sorts. The *gamine* was an independent, mischievous child socialized for early separation. The *chupagrueso* was a dependent and abused victim, willfully pushed out of a dysfunctional family unit. Prepubescent youths were observed to develop chumships or intimate and enduring friendships with a peer, which provided corrective life experiences for children otherwise deprived.

Adolescence forced changes in the youths as they lost the tolerance of adult society and the ability to elicit adults' sympathy and support. *Desamperados* were adolescents who were coping poorly. *Sobrevivientes* were wounded survivors who were coping marginally, whereas the *afortunados* were youths who in adolescence were making a successful adjustment to life. Aptekar (1988) reported that the children "rarely lived permanently on the streets," but exhibited "movement between home, the streets, and a variety of programs" (pp. 37-38). The youths evinced two forms of group life: the *camada* which evolved to provide friendship and support for the younger children, "a personal space to call home" (p. 181); and the *gallada* which was an economic association of younger and older children who shared work and resources to their mutual advantage.

Aptekar (1988) concluded that street children "existed outside the accepted role of childhood" (p. 45), in that they earned and spent money as they saw fit, traveled at will, lived away from home, and controlled their own activities, education, and relationships. Their deviance from accepted norms engendered conflict with adults who anticipated control of and obedience from children. In exploring the extended boundaries of childhood that street children manifested, Aptekar posed the provoking question, whether street children embodied "the impoverished end of childhood, or expanded possibilities" (p. 211).

Palenski and Launer (1987) reported on a qualitative investigation of runaways they conducted in the late 1970s. Data were collected through interviews, participant accounts, and group discussions; informants were recruited from a variety of social service agencies. A majority of respondents had left home due to "problems with parents" (p. 348). Palenski and Launer characterized the runaway experience as being a "social process of action and reaction which unfolds over time" (p. 348), a process labeled by other researchers as a "career" (Becker, 1963; Covenant House New Jersey, 1990c; Irwin, 1970). Implicit in the Palenski and Launer study was the assumption that runaways departed viable families whereas later studies have indicated that many street youths lack viable homes to which they might return (Citizens' Committee, 1983; Crystal, 1986; Los Angeles County Task Force, 1988; Office of the Inspector General, 1983).

Nevertheless, Palenski and Launer's (1987) model has relevance to the present study. *Family disengagement* and the youths' perceptions of *shrinking alternatives* commonly preceded the runaway act. Intervention by family court or a psychologist, which many youths viewed as a violation of the parent-child relationship, precipitated several runaway episodes by their informants.

Upon leaving their homes, the youths commonly experienced ambivalence and uncertainty which Palenski and Launer (1987) termed *managing the residuals*. Identification as a runaway finally required adoption of runaway concerns and a giving up of family concerns. Palenski and Launer identified four issues or themes central to the runaway's existence.

Making it, Getting over, Recognizing emergencies, and *Perfection and control* described the youths' efforts to sustain their existence, deceive authority, organize priorities, and achieve mastery of their environments. Upon remaining away from home and establishing independent lives, the youths identified themselves and were identified by others as fulfilling the role of *runaway.*

Palenski and Launer (1987) gained knowledge of their informants' lives through retrospective accounts rather than direct observation in the field. Though elaborating valuable aspects of the youths' experiences, their study also lacked the texture and timbre which naturalistic field research may provide.

Roberts (1982b) elaborated a four level typology of runaways based on in-depth interviews with runaways, nonrunaways, and selected parents. The *runaway explorer, runaway social pleasure seeker,* and *runaway manipulator* were generally well-adjusted youths who returned home after a short period. *Runaway retreatists* and *endangered runaways* reported significant levels of family conflict and frequent and heavy drug or alcohol use immediately prior to running away. Roberts concluded that the latter two groups were the most vulnerable to the vicissitudes of the streets. Like Palenski and Launer (1987), Roberts based his findings on retrospective accounts by his informants, rather than field observation. Few of his informants remained undomiciled at the time of his contact with them.

In a similar model, Orten and Soll (cited in Miller, Eggertson-Tacon & Quigg, 1990, p. 272), proposed a typology that identified three types of runaways:

The *first degree runners* were youth who were minimally alienated from family members. The *second degree runners* had more street experience and were ambivalent about returning home. *Third degree runners* were older teenagers who identified with the street culture and had no motivation for treatment or to return home. (p. 272)

Staying on the Streets

A central issue for investigators involved with street kids is the persistence of these youths in the street lifestyle, despite its many hazards. A number of researchers have posited explanations for the powerful dynamic which manifests as the youths' addiction to the streets.

Wilkinson (1987) propounded the theory of *secondary socialization* (Berger & Luckmann, cited in Wilkinson, 1987)[1] as a key to this problem. Wilkinson concluded that the act of running away signified a break in the process of primary socialization normally effected by the family of origin, a pattern also suggested by Adams et al. and others (Clark, 1992; Crespi & Sabatelli, 1993; De'Ath & Newman, 1987; Holdaway & Ray, 1992; McCarthy & Hagan, 1992). Children left home in search of community and acceptance, finding on the streets youths from similarly disordered homes, with whom they enacted a process of secondary socialization.

V. Price (1989) and Saltonstall (1984) argued that the loneliness, depression, and low self-esteem which impelled youths to the streets were exacerbated and perpetuated by the violence and betrayal they experienced on the streets. These dynamics were thought to alienate the youths further and to diminish whatever initiative they might have to quit the streets. V. Price indicated that street youths might be reclaimed with years of sustained intervention and support. Saltonstall commented that the youths who used their agency services for other than survival needs demonstrated motivation to change their lifestyles and might be assisted in this through the development of trusting relationships, immediate and supportive responses to the youths' crises, assistance with problem solving, and a respectful and caring attitude. She noted further that if appropriate assistance was available at precisely the point of perceived need when a young man or woman was suddenly "just plain 'fed up' with being on the streets and all it involved" (p. 15), that youths might be helped to change radically.[2]

The addiction literature points to another possible interpretation for youths' remaining on the streets. Beyond a certain threshold, addiction is said to be a primary illness, in which the acquisition and use of the addictive substance becomes all important (American Psychiatric Association, 1987; Skodol, 1989). Seen in this light, the streets might represent the means to an end, enabling the youths to procure sufficient funds to sustain the drug addiction and affording a milieu sympathetic to illicit drug use.

Aptekar (1988) indicated that a variety of factors determined whether a particular Colombian adolescent would remain in a life of delinquency or reenter the mainstream. Aptekar stated that the ultimate outcomes for individual youths were "dependent on the youths' relationships to their homes, the extent and quality of their friendships, their self-concepts and desire to become adult-like, the amount of peer, extended family, benefactor, and institutional support available, the public's reaction to the way they looked, and luck" (p. 84)[3]. Aptekar further noted that because Colombia's street children "lived outside the accepted role of childhood," their options for support were limited. No place existed within the society for independent children, who were a source of dissonance to the ruling class.

Resilient Children

I cite research on *resilient children* here to provide a background for comparison with street youths. Resilient children, those who thrive despite extreme adversity and stress, have been shown to share a number of qualities. Bowlby (1966) was among the first of researchers to note the apparent immunity of some children to psychological injury. He posited that genetic endowment or the child's comeliness or personal appeal might elicit special attention from caregivers.

Subsequently, other researchers observed that these children demonstrated the dispositional attributes of industry, self-sufficiency, constructive problem solving, optimism, faith, imagination, creativity, cooperation, a good self-image, positive self-regard, and a sense of detachment from stressful surroundings (Sundelin-Wahlsten, 1985; Werner, 1989). In addition, resilient children possessed the ability to elicit positive responses from family and strangers (Werner, 1984) and were capable of prolonged intimacy with significant others. Most had had a close bond with a caregiver dating from early infancy (Werner, 1984). In another study, Werner (1989) found that supportive family ties and external support systems were also characteristic of children he called invincible. In contrast, Feitel, Margetson, Chamas, and Lipman (1992) indicated that most of their respondents "had never experienced the influence of a stable caring adult" (p. 158).

Boyar (1986) and Stefanidis, Pennbridge, MacKenzie, and Poltharst (1992) studied the effects of early patterns of attachment on stabilization among runaways and street kids in care. They concluded that runaways with more favorable attachment histories were more amendable to stabilization and reintegration into the mainstream than were those who had experienced chaotic attachments.

The qualities resilient children evince despite adverse circumstances are in marked contrast to the emotional impoverishment, poor self-esteem, and diminished mastery of the environment observed in street kids.

Critique of Literature

Extant research on street kids exhibits several limitations. The preponderance of studies were conducted with homogeneous samples, characterized by Caucasian middle and working class runaways from suburban settings, which do not reflect this country's overall runaway population. Palenski and Launer (1987) examined a more diverse population, one predominantly comprised of Black and Hispanic urban youths. Weisberg (1985) studied domiciled and homeless youths in several urban centers, but her informants were predominantly Caucasian.

Most of the researchers cited obtained respondents through runaway shelters or other youth-oriented agencies such as detention facilities and adolescent psychiatric units. Of the studies reviewed above, few undertook research in the field and only Wilkinson (1987) and Aptekar (1988) focused exclusively on street youths.

Most of the research I had occasion to read as I perused the literature assumed a psychopathological orientation, viewing the runaway as deviant or disturbed. In contrast, the researchers cited above used a socioanthropologic framework which viewed runaway and homeless youths as integral with the family and community. The runaway act was thus examined as a manifestation of interpersonal dynamics. In this context, the runaway act was viewed as a healthy response to an intolerable situation (Adams & Munro, 1979). This world view is congruent with the belief of qualitative researchers that human behavior is best understood in the context in which it occurs (LoBiondo-Wood & Haber, 1990).

This review of literature has summarized qualitative research findings about runaway and street youths and articulated current understanding of why street kids persist in the street lifestyle. Of note is the absence of detailed information about the mundane activities in which street youths engage pursuant to their existence on the streets, the unique knowledge which enables their survival, and the values and attitudes which they manifest. In the next chapter I articulate the rationale for my choice of methodology and outline the strategy I used to explore and elaborate these activities and knowledge.

Notes

1. Similarly in Adams et al., 1985.

2. Similarly in Sereny, 1985.

3. Similarly in Boyar, 1986.

III

Method of Inquiry

Introduction

My purposes were to elaborate the experiences of a small group of street youths, to see the world through their eyes, and to develop an understanding of the activities and relationships which structure and color their existence. The focus or research question was "What are the lived experiences of a small group of street youths?" Data collection was effected through the basic ethnographic techniques of participant observation and informant inquiry. Principles of qualitative analysis were used to guide data analysis and to identify patterns and themes representative of the lives of the youths studied.

Rationale for the Method

A review of the literature about runaway and homeless youths suggested that the runaway or nomadic lifestyle is a complex phenomenon that has not been fully apprehended. The bulk of research on runaway and homeless youths focused on their past histories and their personality attributes. There is a paucity of research exploring the lived experiences of such youths or the meanings they assign to their experiences (Caton, 1986; Kaplan, 1989; Palenski & Launer, 1987).

Researchers have identified the limitations of conventional research methods in understanding the complexities of the runaway experience. Adams and Munro (1979), Bond, Mazin, and Jiminez (1992), Goldmeier and Dean (1973),

Kufeldt and Nimmo (1987), Palenski and Launer (1987), and M.J. Robertson (1989) have recommended that nontraditional research approaches, particularly those that seek apprehension of youths' subjective experiences, be employed to gain greater understanding of the lifestyles of these youths. Qualitative methods do not "seek to reveal causal relationships, but rather to reveal the nature of phenomena as humanly experienced" (Parse, Coyne, & Smith, 1985, p. 16). Leininger (1985) indicated that "the totality of a human lifestyle" (p. 39) is best known through qualitative inquiry, which she defined as

> methods and techniques of observing, documenting, analyzing, and interpreting attributes, patterns, and meanings of specific, contextual, or gestaltic features of phenomena under study. (p. 5)

Lothian (1989) stated that "the ethnographic approach to research examines phenomena in depth and over time, as they actually unfold" (p. 4). Qualitative research methods provide a way to study street youths in their natural setting with the nuances of expression, language, and behavior intact. The use of this method is consistent with the purpose of the study and the need for further research identified by previous authors.

Fieldwork

Selection of Site

Reinharz (1983) indicated that the research method is "determined by the unique characteristics of the field setting" (p. 171). The formal setting, a runaway shelter and crisis center, hereafter called the Center, was one of fortuitous circumstance, given my acquaintance with the agency, its proximity to my own residence, and the number of street kids residing in the area. I had further determined, after three years of experience with street kids, that working with an outreach team would allow me to observe the youths in their preferred locales and activities with a measure of protection and safety. Several local agencies fielded such outreach teams. I ultimately chose to work with the Center, which pioneered work with homeless and runaway adolescents and continues to serve large numbers of displaced and estranged youths every year. The Center has operated an outreach program for several years in an effort to reach those youths who are most alienated. The outreach program is composed of a varying number of staff and volunteers who conduct work with youths at an off-site outreach office and in public areas frequented by needy youths. Two teams of staff members or volunteers travel to areas street youths are known to frequent. These areas, together with the Center and the Outreach Office, constituted the actual setting of my study.

Gaining Access

After favorable contacts with *gate-keepers* at three local youth service agencies, I negotiated access at a runaway shelter situated near the center of a large city. Approval for the research was granted by the agency's administration and newly established Institutional Review Board.

Data Collection

Data Collection Techniques

Participant observation refers to "research characterized by a period of intense social interaction between the researcher and informants, in the milieu of the latter" (McCall & Simmons, cited in Bogdan & Taylor, 1975, p. 5), for the purpose of understanding that milieu. Participant observation combines the receptive attitudes of watching and listening with the more active roles of questioning and asking (Lofland & Lofland, 1984). Informal and intensive interviewing are in many respects integral with participant observation, each involving sustained personal contact with informants as the researcher seeks elucidation of observations and emerging themes (Ely, Anzul, Friedman, Garner, & Steinmetz, 1991; Lofland & Lofland, 1984).

I engaged in participant observation with concurrent interviews of street youths for an initial period of eight months, augmented some months later by additional field observations and interviews. Traveling by van with outreach workers, I visited the field for three to five hours once a week. The nocturnal rhythms of these youths required that such trips occur in the late evening and early morning hours. In the field, I interacted with the youths as circumstances allowed, serving beverages and sandwiches, talking casually with informants, watching, and listening. When I could do so unobtrusively, I questioned the youths further about what I had seen and heard. This sort of informal interview, "on the hoof" so to speak, flows from the situation and from the ongoing analysis of field notes (Ely et al., 1991) and generates "rich, detailed materials" (Lofland & Lofland, 1984, p. 12) essential to a full understanding of the research concern. Weber (1986), speaking of conversation occurring within the interview, elaborated on this dynamic:

> The rapid outpouring of words escapes the track we set it, revealing ambiguities, confusion, variety, and paradox, offering an authentic mosaic of perceptions and thoughts, and providing a sort of window to the consciousness. (p. 70)

Intensive interviews, also called depth or informant interviews, were undertaken at one to two week intervals during the latter stages of data collection to gain more complete pictures of the youths' lives and experiences and to clarify and elaborate on emerging patterns or themes (Guba, 1981). Subject to the youths' temporal constraints, follow-up interviews were conducted to probe particular facets of street life as these were highlighted in the analysis of the first interviews.

Purposive sampling, requisite abilities of youths to inform, and propinquity directed my selection of informants. Specifically, youths of varied backgrounds, experience, orientation, and attitudes within the study's age limitations were selected for interviewing. All the youths I approached for interviews assented and most did so enthusiastically.[1] This strategy yielded four female and six male informants of differing ethnic, socioeconomic, and sexual identification and orientation. This group mirrored the street population I observed. Interview informants were *insiders* who were capable of providing and communicating accurate information and perceptions about their world (Spradley, 1979; Knaack, 1984). A small number of informants was sought, consistent with the premise that the optimal number of informants in qualitative studies may be very limited (Omery, 1983, cited in Cobb & Hagemaster, 1987; Reinharz, 1983). I interviewed three youths informally at length while in the field and interviewed seven more youths in a more formal setting. Four informants were interviewed formally on two or more occasions.

A list of possible interview questions[2] was designed to explore the experiences of informants, to elicit information about emerging themes, and to elaborate on questions or gaps suggested by the data. These questions served as the take-off point for some interviews and were used further as situations indicated.

Successful interviewing, according to Spradley (1979),

> is predicated upon 'asking questions, listening
> instead of talking, taking a passive rather than an
> assertive role, expressing verbal interest in the
> other person, and showing interest by eye contact
> and other nonverbal means. ' (p. 46)

The abilities required of qualitative interviewers are consonant
with those required of nurses (Cobb & Hagemaster, 1987),
skills I had sharpened in my years of nursing experience and
education.

I conducted most interviews in secluded areas of
restaurants near the Center. On a few occasions, I interviewed
informants in neighboring parks or in a comfortable private
office in the Center, according to the convenience and wishes
of the informants. I sought to maintain the privacy of the
informant, but because of street noise, pedestrian traffic, and
other interruptions, no location proved ideal.

Audiotaping interviews presented a challenge as well. One
informant, Sarah, lost her usual exuberance and spontaneity in
the presence of the tape recorder. Interviews with two youths
proved nearly inaudible due to their diction and strong local
inflection. On two occasions, interviews were lost because of
malfunctioning equipment, notwithstanding my most diligent
precautions.

The data gathering process was concluded when I felt, as
Reinharz (1983) suggested, "saturated, depleted, complete"
(p. 181). This feeling coincided with saturation of themes and
redundancy in the data (Ely et al., 1991; Lincoln & Guba,
1985).

Interviews were taped subject to the consent of informants[3] and transcribed by a legal secretary of my acquaintance, in accordance with the constraints of confidentiality and protection of clients. Preservation of tapes, discs and transcripts is described in Protection of Informants.

Recording Data

I wrote my observations as soon as possible after a field visit, usually the next morning. Brief notes taken in or just after leaving the field together with purposeful recollection of key words were used to reconstruct in the log the conversations and activities I observed. These notations included "descriptions of people, objects, places, events, activities, and conversations" (Bogdan & Biklen, 1982, p. 74) I had observed. Specifically, I described the areas in which I traveled, the people I saw, and their activities, interactions, and conversations. In addition, I attempted to capture the gestalt of situations, as when violence was observed, or a striking stillness or synergy manifested. My ability to recall and record conversations and impressions gained in the field was affirmed as I submitted samples of logs to other observers for evaluation of credibility.

I also employed the log to record my impressions, reflections, and personal reactions regarding the field work, the research process, and my informants. This practice allows the researcher to relate the subjective and objective dimensions of the research process such that each dimension informs the other (Ely et al., 1991; Lipson, 1984; Reinharz, 1983). A substantial proportion of the log described my interactions with outreach staff and their observations of the kids. Other notations related to ongoing turmoil at the Center and my difficulties balancing personal, professional, and academic responsibilities.

Protection of Informants

The observation of street youths is by nature a sensitive undertaking (Sereny, 1985), as these are vulnerable youths engaging in nonnormative activities. I had previously established a high degree of rapport and trust with affected youths in my work at the Center. My commitment to the welfare of these youths outweighed my investment in the research and I made every effort in my research to protect the youths and my relationships with them. The observational facet of the study was nonintrusive and involved participant observation and informal interviewing in public areas. I neither sought nor recorded identifying data. It is of note that street youths are rarely known by their given names (McCarthy & Hagan, 1992) and seldom have a forwarding address. I informed youths with whom I engaged in conversation that I was conducting research on street kids and inquired the age of the youths. Any youth who reported he or she was seventeen or younger at the time of the study was excluded from consideration except for one minor youth, Sarah, whose mother agreed to her participation. When I engaged in direct and substantive conversation with youths during field visits, I further explained the research[4] and sought written or verbal consent from the youths for their participation.[5] I explained to the youths that their participation was voluntary and anonymous and could be terminated at any time without repercussion.

Intensive interviews differed from field observations in that conversations were purposeful and probed sensitive areas. I explained to youths that my purpose was "to learn what it's like for a kid on the street," that their participation was voluntary, that they could withdraw at any time without penalty, and that I would use pseudonyms and disguise other details throughout all written materials to maintain their confidentiality and anonymity. Many youths, to my surprise, objected to anonymity, but were advised that it was a condition of participation. Youths were advised they could review materials pertaining to them at will. If the youth agreed to participate, I obtained that person's written consent.[6]

Two youths who became distressed during our interviews indicated, as did Lipson's (1984) and Sereny's (1985) informants, that the opportunity to talk to a concerned person about their feelings and experiences had been of considerable benefit. In a few instances, I felt the inclusion of sensitive data might threaten a youth's welfare and so deleted that material from review.

All research materials, including tapes, transcripts, logs, and floppy discs were preserved in locked containers in a secure location. Audiotapes and discs were erased upon successful completion of the manuscript. Copies of the completed work are available at the Center and the Outreach Office for interested youths.

Trustworthiness and the Stance of the Researcher

Qualitative research diverges in many respects from quantitative research. One concern in my study was the issue of researcher bias which may affect the ability of the researcher as instrument to observe, assimilate, and portray the world of the informant credibly. Reinharz (1983) suggested that by examining "their own previous experiences, intentions, hopes, and prejudices to try to understand what they are bringing to the study" (p. 175), researchers could minimize this effect. In examining my feelings and attitudes about street kids and my relation to them, I sought to acknowledge and explore those notions which might affect my ability to perceive phenomena clearly.

I discerned early in my employment at the runaway shelter not only that these youths engaged my interest, but that I felt a certain kinship with them, having been an outsider of one sort or another most of my life. I remain drawn to them, notwithstanding that I left that employment some months ago. A number of researchers have noted that sincere concern for (Weber, 1986), personal and professional interest in (Ely et al., 1991), and a "genuine relation with informants" (Reinharz, 1981, p. 417) enhanced rather than diminished the credibility of research findings.

It is frequently argued that a researcher should not undertake research within his or her own agency or environment, as preconceptions about the area and prior knowledge of one's informants may intrude on an accurate representation of that world (Bogdan & Taylor, 1975). Lipson (1984) indicated that in her experience as a clinician, peer, and researcher, "each role informed the other to produce a richness of data not otherwise available to a researcher having only one perspective" (p. 351). Further, though my employment at the runaway shelter joined me to other staff, health care providers in particular, it did not necessarily confer "insider" status with respect to street kids. I was, at most I believe, a *trusted other*, as distinct from Freidman's *intimate acquaintance* (Ely et al., 1991). I did not share in the activities and attitudes that defined street life, but I accepted the youths unconditionally as they disclosed themselves to me. I took genuine pleasure in their company, showed interest in their concerns and activities, and expressed concern for their welfare. They in turn reciprocated my affection, directed their peers to me, and sought to protect me from the vagaries of the street. That I should seek to study their ways of being in the world was interpreted as a natural extension of my longstanding interest in their lives and experiences, to which they eagerly assented.

My empathy was an asset in my research in that it enabled me to develop rapport with my informants, engage their point of view (Ely et al., 1991), and intuit their feelings and perspectives with little difficulty. Ely et al. honor this tacit knowledge as a product of meaningful lived experience.

Aptekar (1988) described two forms of distortion to which observers of Colombia's street children were prone. In the first form, researchers portrayed the children as victims and the researcher as hero. In its opposing form, children were viewed as heros and the researcher as a voyeur, so to speak, who took vicarious pleasure in the child's exploits. Aptekar attributed these responses to the contradiction inherent in the idea of independent children. My own field notes reflected this struggle as I identified in myself a tendency to focus on the more dramatic aspects of street life. I was also aware that my informants' adventures provoked in me a degree of vicarious satisfaction. These responses, which Lipson (1984) and Reinharz (1983) indicated provide vital clues to data analysis, proved particularly important in my analysis of transvestite street kids and a few individual youths.

Finally, I was aware in my employment and subsequently in my field work that a few of my more irascible contacts elicited a certain antipathy in me. I perceived three or four youths over the years to be histrionic, manipulative or provocative to an extreme. This had a negative influence on my ability to interact with them effectively. Only one of my informants, whom I have called Teddy, provoked this response in me. On our first meeting, I was able through conscious effort to communicate with him empathically. On seeing him subsequently, I chose to avoid him. In retrospect, I believe that my perception of his extreme neediness triggered awareness of my own vulnerability and elicited my withdrawal. As I reflect now on my reaction I believe it is probable that such responses perpetuated Teddy's neediness and isolation.

Trustworthiness, the credibility of my representation of the informants' world to outsiders and ethical considerations such as protection of informants' privacy and integrity, were also of concern to me, my informants, and my audience. The following paragraphs address these issues.

Trustworthiness of a naturalistic endeavor may be judged, according to Guba (1981), by its credibility, transferability, dependability, and confirmability. Lincoln and Guba (1985) suggested several strategies supportive of trustworthiness, tersely summarized by Ely et al. (1991):

> The researcher must: have prolonged engagement in the field, do persistent observation, triangulate, search for negative cases, determine referential adequacy, experience peer debriefing, and check with the people one studied. (p. 96)

Aptekar (1988) noted that using more than one method of data collection reduced the bias of each method, observing in multiple situations reduced the bias of observations,[7] and the use of secondary sources increased the scope of information.

At periodic intervals throughout the data collection and analysis, I submitted the emergent work to various informants for comment and criticism. These lunch meetings elicited enthusiasm and serious thought by youths who were unaccustomed to having someone solicit their ideas. The process engendered a sense of collaboration and purpose among participants, effects said to invest the research with greater meaning and credibility (Reinharz, 1983).

In the subsequent refining of ideas and writing stages I had some difficulty locating previous contacts, who, in keeping with expectations, had dispersed. I was compelled therefore to locate other youths of similar inclinations and lifestyles to respond to the work-in-progress. Member checker comments are included in my analysis as appropriate. I have used popular and scholarly literature to corroborate my observations and impressions and the interpretations of other researchers to support or challenge my own conclusions.

The function of peer debriefing was fulfilled by a group of peers who were also engaged in qualitative research. The support group and interested colleagues served as interim reviewers or auditors, examining materials and memos periodically for consistency and authenticity. Analytic memos provided a further accounting as I noted insights and emerging interpretations and reflected on my feelings, concerns, frustrations, and successes.

Data Analysis

Data analysis refers to that process whereby "recorded experiences, conversation transcripts, pieces of information are compiled, reduced, and examined for their interactions (patterns) and basic themes" (Reinharz, 1983, p. 182). Data analysis, according to Ely et al. (1991), is an idiosyncratic proposition. No single formula can enable the researcher to construct hypotheses and recognize themes (Bogdan & Taylor, 1975). Rather, the complex interplay between researcher, informants, and data ferments according to "the knowledge, insight, and imagination" (Ely et al., p. 147) of the researcher, ultimately yielding a document uniquely reflective of the informants as realized by the *researcher as instrument*. Nevertheless, the tenets of analysis elaborated by Carini (cited in Ely, 1984), with modifications by Ely, guided the process of discovery as I sought meaning in the data. These steps are described below:

1. *Development of detailed knowledge of content of interview and logs*. Through repeated listening to audiotapes and reading of transcripts and logs, I became familiar with the content of the material.

2. *Noting impressions.* During this process, I noted initial impressions of the data, which served as a frame of reference for later comparisons.

3. *Listing of tentative headings.* On the basis of the repeated review of the data in Step One, headings that reflected recurring ideas were established as a tentative organization of the thoughts expressed in the interview and log material.

4. *Reflective analysis.* The relationship between the impressions noted in Step Two and the headings established in Step Three were examined to clarify and refine the headings.

5. *Organization of data.* Through listening to audiotapes and rereading transcripts and logs, I grouped data under the established category headings. In this return to the raw data, new impressions were noted and revisions made of headings generated in Step Three as indicated.

6. *Listing of data by heading.* Verbatim statements of subjects and observations derived from logs and interviews were listed under appropriate headings so that headings were linked with the data from which they emerged.

7. *Summarizing new impressions.* The results of Step Six were studied and new insights noted.

8. *Establishing themes.* Themes were written which described patterns, observations, or perspectives reflective of a particular informant or quality noted in the data.

9. *Integrating data.* The frameworks, substantiating information and themes for each informant or quality were conjoined so that the range of elements could be observed.

10. *Comparison of data.* The commonalities and differences in related elements were examined (pp. 6-7).

Data analysis commenced with the record of the first field visit, as I immersed myself in the log. By writing comments in the margins of the log and asking myself what segments of data represented, I was able to develop tentative headings. This process continued with subsequent log entries, as I compared earlier and later impressions. Recurring patterns or ideas were identified, which served to order the data. Questions or gaps emerging in the data guided interviews which I conducted as data analysis progressed. Upon completion of each interview, I listened to the audiotape and read the transcript, processing this data as I did the field notes. As I listed new impressions and ideas, I tested these against older material, revising headings and refining categories as indicated. Occasionally, as I reflected on the data, I discerned new patterns or meanings or relationships in the data. I took advantage of these moments to write analytic memos, exploring these ideas and trying new interpretations.

As I proceeded, I organized data by category, literally cutting and filing sections of data in labeled folders. Related and overlapping materials were filed in one folder, for example, the folder I labeled *Family* contained data pertaining to several subcategories: Family Background, Abuse by Family, Family Conflict, Relationships with Family, and Loss of Family Members. On occasion, data reflected more than one category, such that Relationships with Family was cross-referenced in the *Relationship* folder. After identifying categories, I listed these and sought to cluster related elements within broader *metacognitions*, and define relationships among the various elements. At periodic intervals, I reviewed the data and analysis to reflect on the totality of my efforts and weigh the correspondence between the two. This process continued throughout the data collection, concluding with the final analysis and writing stages, in which I elaborated themes representative of the youths, described relationships among identified elements and integrated my observations and impressions in a unifying model.

Researcher Stress

My research was undertaken at a time of considerable stress personally and professionally. As a single parent, I was responsible for the support and welfare of a preteen child and the homemaking that entailed. I was fortunate during prolonged periods of field work, data entry, and analysis, to have friends who were willing to take Lara for overnight and weekend stays.

My work at the Center was fulfilling as it had always been; however, extreme administrative turmoil occurring as I undertook my research was of some consequence as it generated intense anxiety and instability within the institution. This charged atmosphere preoccupied and distracted Center staff and rendered my research more difficult than it might otherwise have been.

Support Group

My engagement with supportive groups and individuals offered necessary support and direction throughout the research process. My peer support group included Michael Boyle and Dorit Amir, who had been my classmates in graduate school. We met at frequent intervals thereafter, sharing camaraderie over our respective research endeavors. As we commiserated over the frustrations of travel, course work, family responsibilities, and the demands of qualitative research, we gained strength and the courage to carry on. In the group we reviewed one another's logs, tried out new ideas, and argued alternate points of view. Because our disciplines and research concerns varied, we were exposed to the unique knowledge and insights individuals brought to the group, a dynamic which enriched our analytic perspectives. The group process served to engender credibility in our research, as biases and distortions were confronted and explored and interpretations were sounded and argued.

My colleagues John Phillips, Margot Ely, and Judith Lothian provided persistent encouragement, direction, and instruction as my enthusiasm flagged or obstacles were encountered. Kelly Mayo provided invaluable counsel and sustenance as I struggled with final analysis and writing.

The culmination and substance of this long and arduous process is the articulation of the experiences and beliefs manifested by my informants which follows.

Notes

1. Similarly in Balshem, Oxman, van Rooyen, & Girod, 1992.

2. See Appendix A.

3. See Appendix C.

4. See Appendix B.

5. See Appendix C.

6. See Appendix C.

7. Similarly in Reinharz, 1983.

IV

Setting the Scene:
Introducing the Youths and the Streets

Introduction

As I organized my field notes and interviews, I constructed two levels of analysis and interpretation. The first involved distilling the essence of the stories individual youths told me of their backgrounds, families, and experiences on the streets. The second level involved creating themes which ran through all or many of the stories. These themes relate to street understandings, survival strategies, family and other relationships, self-perceptions, future expectations, drug use, and group life.

My intent in this chapter is to set the scene: by sharing the stories of ten youths, selected from the dozens I came to know as I spent time in the field; by recounting my impressions of the streets; and by presenting my informants' perspectives of the streets. In subsequent chapters, I identify and elaborate the themes which emerged as I assimilated and processed hundreds of pages of field notes, interview transcriptions, and supporting documents.

Portraits of Youths

G.A. Kelly (1955) developed a theory of personal constructs to enable a client and therapist to identify those qualities and beliefs which define the client's world. The psychotherapy client is asked to describe himself or herself in the third person, as a very empathic and intimate friend might describe the individual. The resulting sketch is known as a self-characterization and reflects "how the person structures his immediate world, how he sees himself in relation to these structures and the strategies he has developed to handle his world" (Bannister & Fransella, 1971, p. 79).

The vignettes which follow are not strict self-characterizations as defined by Kelly (cited in Bannister & Fransella, 1971); rather I have employed the Ely et al. (1991) modifications developed for the purpose of thematic analysis. Vignettes and constructs

are distilled from the data in as close a likeness as possible to the participant's mode of expression. The intention is to present in miniature the essence of what the researcher has seen and heard [of the participant] over time. (p. 154)

They are portraits, then, developed in part as I came to know and apprehend the youths' understanding of themselves in relation to the world and in large part from the youths' own disclosures. Ten vignettes are presented, four of females and six of males. I had known several of the youths during my tenure at the Center; which contacts were renewed on the streets. I made the acquaintance of other youths as I engaged in field work. The youths, Black, Causasian, and Hispanic, manifested a diverse range of experience as well: straight, bisexual, and gay; hustlers, prostitutes, and one nonprostitute; crack users, intravenous heroin and cocaine users, and one alcoholic. The stories I recount here are remarkably congruent with those other researchers tell (Powers & Jaklitsch, 1989; Sereny, 1985; Weisberg, 1985), an observation which serves to reinforce both the reality and perseveration of abuse. I offer the vignettes now as a record of each youth's having lived and moved and affected the world and as an introduction to the analysis which follows, so that the reader may share the spirit and pain and uniqueness each youth signifies. I have attempted in these vignettes to write in the cadence and language the youths affect in speaking, to communicate their voices more effectively.

Darryl

Hi. My name is Darryl. Katherine here is my friend, she asked me to describe myself to you. Well, I don't know. I'm a handsome young man, I'm tall with blond hair. The girls all try to come on to me, but I don't pay them no attention. I have a girlfriend, one's all I need. Girlfriends are too much trouble, I end up taking care of them and starving myself. I like to look good and take care of myself, I dress nice. Mary, my counselor, bought me a leather jacket and she's going to get me some boots I think. She's a soft touch. If I want something and don't have the money, I can talk her into getting it for me. My friend says I look like a preppie sometimes when I wear my khaki pants and striped shirt. I don't know about that. I like jeans and T-shirts myself.

My mom is alcoholic. She drank a lot when she was carrying me, so it gave me some trouble. My feet are messed up so I can't find shoes to fit and nobody doesn't want to pay for me to get surgery. I get upset real easy. I didn't do well in school. My dad left us and my mom married this guy, my stepfather. He used to beat me up and throw me around. He would hold me by my feet upside down over the stairs and threaten to drop me, then use me as a shield when the police would come. I was a lot of trouble, tearing up the room and stuff. They put me in foster care and group homes and finally they put me in an institution where they send crazy people. They put me on Thorazine there, made me like a zombie. I hated it. I couldn't move. Those doctors messed me up bad. When I got out on a pass I left, I didn't go back. I wouldn't go back. I guess I've been on the streets since then. Sometimes now I stay with my mom, sometimes I stay with my girlfriend. She has an apartment. She is mentally ill, though. I have to see that she takes her medicine and goes to her doctor. I met her in a bar. She's hard to wake up so sometimes I pour ice water over her head.

I like to go to the movies. I've seen almost everything that comes out. Sometimes I go to the library and read a book. I go to parties a lot. My counselor says I drink a lot, like I'm an alcoholic, but I don't think so. I like to go to nice places to eat dinner too, when I can get the money. My favorite restaurant is Le Chateau. I know the good places. I know how to act, too, and how to use my silverware.

Lately I've been doing things I don't like to do. I do it because I have to and I'm good at it, but I just can't quit. I want to quit and I can't. I break into peoples' houses when they're gone and I take some stuff. The best clothes, this really expensive Alexander Julian shirt I've got on, money and jewelry if I can find any. Then I sneak out. I can pick a lock so you can't tell I was there. Why shouldn't I do it? It's the only thing I do really well, better than anything else.

I've had jobs. I used to work cleaning up at the movies and they would let me in free to see the shows. Sometimes when I need money I hand out flyers. They pay me the minimum wage and I get paid the same day. I panhandle too but that's hard because people are mean to you. I drink when I can get it, but I don't use any drugs or prostitute myself, I just have too much to look forward to.

I keep my stuff in these bags over under the bridge. Mostly nobody bothers it. It's my secret place, sometimes I sleep there. I don't have many friends, just my girlfriend and the people where I go when I'm sick and my counselors at the other place, where they work with homeless kids.

I been in some programs where they try to help you, give you a place to stay, but I get kicked out, 'cause I have a bad temper. I hit the counselor in the face because he tried to tell me what to do and they threw me out, at that program.

When I tried to apply for disability, they refused me. They wanted more proof that I'm a mentally disturbed deranged young man.

My counselors, they try to help me. I've been seeing them for a long time, since I was on the streets. I'm just a young kid and I've never trusted anybody on account of growing up so mistreated, but I am working to accept my counselors so I can let them help me and find me a place to stay.

Junior

So I've been asked to tell you about myself. It's not the first time, I've been on television a few times when people decide they want to learn about street kids.

So, as it happens, my mother had a nervous breakdown right after I was born, then my father he abandoned me when I was three months old. I never met him. I never knew him. It makes me angry that my parents both left me before they ever even knew me. I was in foster care all my life. Three of them before I was thirteen. I stayed the longest with one couple, eight years from when I was five 'til I was thirteen. I loved them the most of all. I left them because I thought they were mistreating me, telling me what to do and stuff. Now I see they weren't so bad. I still try to keep in contact with them, but they won't have anything to do with me because I'm gay.

From thirteen to fifteen, I went through like maybe twenty foster homes. "Looking for love in all the wrong places." I just couldn't see anybody else taking the place of my foster parents

I had lived with for so long. I've been on the streets pretty much all the time since I was fifteen. In '88 I moved around and went to Florida. I would stay in shelters up and down the East Coast. Then in '89, on my birthday, I found Club House New York. The Club House, that's a kind of a shack under the East Side Bridge. Me and some other kids, Rocco, Andy, a bunch of bazooka[1] heads, lived there off and on for a few years. We had mattresses and a grill and boxes for our stuff. We ate really well, stuff we snagged at the store. But mainly we smoked bazooka.

I've used drugs since I was thirteen, marijuana to start with. I had run away and started hanging out with some other Banji Boys. That means a pretty young gay Hispanic boy, smart and funny, like me. We would just get high and dance and listen to music. I started hustling when I was fifteen, sixteen, hanging out on the Wharf, when that was fashionable. I call it "free-lancing the public relations field." You meet a lot of people, all sorts of people, gay men who can pay the bill. I am a proper, good looking kind of guy, I can fit in anywhere, I get the best dates. But I don't know, once a person starts using drugs, they end up just like I did, hustling for the drug. I've been in jail seven times, possession and solicitation mainly.

I started using crack when I was eighteen. I guess it's an escape, to get away from the pain I've suffered throughout my life. I've been in two, three treatment programs. I was in a program and was doing very well but I started learning about myself and that really hurt a lot and I ran from it. Now, it's like I've been out here so long, it's the only life I know.

There's one date I've gone out with since I was seventeen. I've done some bad things to him, stolen from him and used him, but through it all he's been there for me.

I don't have any friends out here, on the streets. Everybody out here, if you've got money, they want to be your friend, take advantage of you. So when I'm out here, I try to avoid other people, I just do my drugs, by myself.

I've been getting bored with it for the longest time. I'm bored with the streets, I'm bored with staying home in friends' apartments. My clients tell me how smart I am, how I don't belong out here. Like I want to hear that. I always try to plan what I'm going to do, go back to school, get a real job, but I plan too much and never follow through. Now I'm just gonna roll with it and see where it takes me . . . There's an old song, "Street Life,"©[2] it describes how I feel.

> I still hang around,
> neither lost nor found.
> Hear the long sounds
>   of music in the night.
>
> Nights are always bright
> That's all the same for me.
> I play the street life
> Because there's no place I can go.
> Street life, it's the only
>   life I know
> Street life, there's a thousand
>   parts to play
> Street life, 'til you
>   play your life away.

---

[2] *Street Life.* Words and music by Joe Sample and Will Jennings © Copyright 1979 by Four Knights Music and Irving Music Co. All rights of Four Knights Music administered by MCA Music Publishing, a Division of MCA, Inc., New York, NY 10019. Used by permission. All rights reserved.

You let the people see
    just who you want to be
And every night you shine
    just like a superstar.
You've got a life to play,
    a ten cent masquerade.
You dress, you walk, you talk
    you're who think you are.

Street life, you can run
    away from time,
Street life, for a nickel
    or a dime,
Street life, but you'd
    better not get old,
Street life, for you're going
    to feel the cold,
There's always love for sale,
    a grown-up fairy tale
Prince Charming always smiles
    behind the silver spoon.[3]
And if you hear them young
    your song is always sung,
Your love will pay your way
    beneath the silver moon.
Street life, street life
Street life, street life.

(Sample & Jennings, 1980)

Sarah

My nurse, Miss Kit Kat I call her, asked me would I talk to you about myself. I told her I would, for the small price of some Reese's Cups. When I get through talking to you, I get my candy. She always keeps candy just for me.

The story starts out, I had a mom, a dad, and brothers and sisters just like everybody. But when I was little, about four years old, I fell out of a window and hurt my head and was in a coma for two months. I have seizures now and have to take Dilantin. When I was six or seven, my real dad disappeared. He's a lucky old goat. He lives across the river and won't nobody give me his address. My mother remarried and my stepfather abused me sexually, that's why I ran the first time, when I was seven. My cousin that I was close to got shot, and now nobody but me ever thinks about him.

When I was coming up, I was always good in school. I got good grades and was on my way to being a dancer or an artist. But I always had to do everything for myself, from when I was eight years old. Fix my own meals, take care of myself. My house, it was like a battlefield, everybody arguing all the time, mainly they were criticizing me. My mom, she abused me all the time. She used to hit me with extension cords or her high-heeled shoe, put me in a cold shower and beat me. She would beat me for three hours at a time. I don't understand why she had to be careful to hit me so much. That's when I started hanging out with my brother's friends and getting high on weed.

Anyway, I was neglected a lot. So many people around the house and I didn't get no attention. My mom acting helpless like she was a little kid, letting everybody run over her, when she wasn't hitting you. When I was twelve I had enough. I seen the streets on TV so I left and went on my own. I been on the streets ever since. My brothers and sisters, they be running away too. But they would always go back home. Me, I saw how you could get what you needed out there. I saw you could make money turning tricks and I started that on my own when I was thirteen. And here on the streets, I was drugging my own self and it wasn't beer and it wasn't weed, it was crack.

I've been in jail more times than you could count. Possession of controlled substances, dealing, solicitation. Most places, I can escape. I just open the door and moonwalk or follow someone out.

I have a little trouble sometimes with my distributors. If I bust out with the merchandise, steal drugs I'm supposed to be selling, like when I stole thirty-nine bundles,[4] I get the daylights beat out of me or run over by a car. Sometimes that shit happens. A car rolled over me, I got knocked down. I go to the hospital and nothing is wrong with me. These other kids getting killed, they mix with the wrong crowd. They're not as smart as I am.

I have a few friends. My best friend is Rhonda. We been together on the streets for three, four years. We help each other out. Her brother Brian, he's on the streets too, he's gay and every time I see him, he's like, "I'll turn straight for you anytime." That's because the guys are hot for me. I have lots of boyfriends, but I always liked the girls, to be exact. I been going out with girls since I was nine. But you can't just run with anybody, you got to be careful on the streets who you talk to, who you are going to trust, 'cause the night has eyes and it will be telling on you.

I have a good time out here, I get the guys to fall in love with me and then I leave 'em crying. Won't nobody own me, ever. See how many people I can take advantage of, take their money and run. Getting high, chasing the dragon, that's the best. I can smoke crack for days at a time, then I go to the Center to crash, get some food and some sleep, get ready for the next expedition.

How I get food is because the guys all want to get close to me. I go in a store and sweet talk the clerk—"Yo, Keith, I'll come back and treat you right." I walk out with $20.00 worth of food but I never do go back and treat them right.

I used to run with a gang, the Dead End Kids. We wore our colors, vests with our names on them. I was the youngest, the only girl. We used to mess with the cops, fuck them up. Every gang member had to kill a cop. See my tattoo, my gang name? "Wild Child."

I was upstate for a while in detention, I did good for a long time. They sent me to visit a group home where I was supposed to go when I was discharged. But I ran and didn't go back, 'cause you could drink there. I might have stayed, but out here I don't have to go to school.

Now I'm just going to live life to the fullest. Take it day by day, every day, party hardy 'cause you just might not make it tomorrow. Have you heard this? "Little Miss Muffet sat off her tuffet, along came a spider, sat down beside her. What did he say? 'What's in the bowl, bitch!'"

I wrote this poem before I left home. Now give me my candy, Katherine.

> One summer morning
>   a robin was at my window.
> I summoned it to my sill
>   with a piece of bread.
> I fed it and patted it.
> Quickly while it was eating
> I went and smashed the window
>   on its frigging head.

Louie

I can talk about myself. I usually keep it all in, but
sometimes it helps to talk about it, to the right person.
Someone who won't think less of you 'cause you exposed your
self, your real self, what a lousy past you had. My life was
pretty fucked up. I was born upstate, but my real parents were
killed in a plane crash when I was a baby. I was adopted when
I was a few months old. My old man's a neurologist. He abused
me sexually, mentally, physically, throughout my childhood.
When I was two, he picked me up and threw me across the
bedroom because I didn't know how to do something. When I
was four, I remember going to the hospital to get my head
stapled because I didn't know how to buckle my pants up. He
got mad and he hit me over the head with his cast, he had a
cast on his arm, and he hit me over the head with it. It's so
stupid, because I didn't know how to buckle my pants up. He
slammed the car door on me, broke my nose, because he was
pissed off about something. It was one thing or another all my
life.

When I was older, seven or eight, they was in a divorce
proceeding and he wanted to get information out of me so he
tied my hands up, had me in the bedroom and he abused me
sexually and verbally. He sat on me, he snapped three of my
fingers. I can hardly believe it all really happened. Such
perverts, treating me like I was nothing. They treated the dog
better than they did me.

My older brother and sister, they were adopted too. But
they weren't abused. It was just me. I got picked out. They
used to tell me, "You're nothing. You'll never become anything.
You, you're a low life, you're nothing." They didn't take care of
me. I did everything. When I was eight or nine, the courts
figured things out and sent me away for four years. Then I
started getting home visits and everything was OK for a while,

you know, what are they going to do? So they treated me right, gave me everything I wanted, trying to show the judge they had changed. So the court let me out when I was 12 and bingo, things started to happen again. They just treated me so bad, criticizing me, abusing me, not even knowing anything about me, fucking with my head. So I started to hang out on the corner, sniffing heroin, running some bundles, getting into drugs. I'd sniff the heroin and I'd go home and I could handle what was going on. Then I was doin' it more and more and somebody introduced me to the needle. When I was 13, I shot a bag of dope. I never went back to sniffing after that. Shooting is the best high. My parents could hit me with baseball bats, I wouldn't care. They knew I was doing it. But they didn't care two shits about me.

They gave everything to the other two. Whatever they wanted, they got, whatever they needed, they got. If I did something, it was "Yeah, he did it, no doubt about it." I'm wrong, you know what I mean? It was like I was in the corner all my life. I never had anybody I could talk to. So I started getting more aggressive as I got older, harder, more cold hearted. It didn't bother me that my parents abused me or when I saw other people get hurt. Sometimes I even hurt them. When I was 14, I got busted. I kept probation for a couple of months, then I started screwing up. Dope was getting to me. So I was sent upstate for 22 months. It's like I've been in jail most of my life.

When I came out, I had no education. I went home and they wanted to put me in ninth grade. Seventeen years old, can you see me in ninth grade? So I didn't really care. I was like in a separate world all day long. I couldn't handle all the classes, like going from one to another all day long like normal people. It wasn't in my brain. I was always sat in one classroom all my life.

After I was home for a while, I got in a fight with my dad and smashed him up with a baseball bat. His car too. The judge listened to me for a change and they sent me to a job program, nonsecure detention, the only break I ever had. They had me building a house while I was up there and getting paid for it. It wasn't like I was being punished. They put me to work and paid me for it. I took Culinary Arts, got my GED with an almost perfect score and my driver's license. I got everything now. I'm lucky I beat up my old man. If I didn't, I would never have gotten to go to the job program. It was the best experience in my whole life.

I was still using drugs heavy duty though. Had my friends bringing drugs into the program for me. I had a needle under my radiator. I work better on heroin. Then I came out. I had my girl, she got pregnant. Her father wanted to kill me, chased me around with a sawed off shotgun. She's gonna be a cop, she's in the Police Academy now. My daughter, she's two and a half now, she's beautiful. I see them all the time, we just don't live together. I guess she wants to see me straight before she agrees to a permanent situation.

So I got a job, then I fucked up 'cause I was on drugs. I was consuming $200 a day, easy. I had to do a lot of prostitution for that shit, staying out all night for days at a time. I'd go out robbing the faggots too, I hate faggots. So I'm on methadone maintenance now. It's not good for me, but it helps me forget the pain and I need it. And at least it keeps me off the streets, out of jail.

I never went back to my parents. I haven't seen them for five years. I never want to see them again. I don't hang out with people. I don't ask nobody for nothing. There's nobody I trust, nobody I want to get to know. Sometimes I go to a drop in center, sometimes I visit my woman, the one that's got my daughter. I guess I trust her sometimes.

I get by. I have a subsidized apartment. I deal some drugs, sometimes I'll snatch some of the crack back. I rob. I love to rip off necklaces, gold from the johns. I guess I'm a pretty angry dude, huh. I hustle too, men and women both. Sometimes I get young boys for old men, that's good money.

But the winter is coming. I'm trying to get myself together, changing things. Hopefully by this time next year, I'll have a whole different future. My heart is going strong. My real parents left me a fortune, I can collect pretty soon. I'm gonna get my daughter, take up with my woman. 'Cause she loves me. I always had everything, it's just that I got to do everything on my own.

Rocco

So you want to know about us street kids, huh.

Do we get a percentage on the book?

Do we get to go on TV with you?

Really now, this is privileged information. I don't talk to just anybody. But I guess you're not just anybody.

It all started, see, with a normal family. But that didn't last long. My aunt mostly raised me because my parents didn't get along. My mom left when I was three and then I got shifted from one family to the next, all over the States, for a long time. When I was with one aunt, my cousin, he was 12, 13 years old, he molested me for several years. I started running away, but that's when I found out I was gay, 'cause he found a girlfriend and it bothered me. My family, they're real religious, and when they found out I was gay, it's been nothing but trouble ever since.

The first time I left home, my mom, my aunt, you know what I mean, had given me twenty dollars to go shopping to buy some clothes, and this gay guy started following me around the mall and I was terrified. But we got to talking and instead of abusing me he helped me and I moved in with him for a long time, off and on for seven years. My family was like, "What?!!" 'cause I was so young and all. We are still good friends, even though we've never had a sexual relationship. He was like a father, what I know about the gay world and how to protect myself, he taught me. He was very strict with me.

When I was fifteen, I got involved in the pier scene, vougueing and all. All the gay kids, Black and Latino, and even some straight kids on the weekends, we used to hang out on the Wharf, listening to music and dancing and stuff. I learned to vogue and was good enough I won prizes in the Balls. Plus I'm real cute and fresh and people like to be around me. Back then, it meant security. You had to be in a House[5] in order to fit in with the crowd. It was like a family to me, my family away from home, my gay family. It used to be a lot of fun years ago. It's just dangerous now, all the drugs and rivalries. People will stab you for a trophy they wanted.

My dad was always sick after my mother left. He committed suicide a year and a half ago. My mother still blames herself. Till she left, he worked two jobs and we had everything. If maybe she would have stuck it out, we could have had everything, and we probably could have been "normal kids." Instead, my sister got killed on the streets and I'm still out here.

I started turning tricks when I was 15, when I came out. But it wasn't so intense then. You did it once in a while, you got a lot of money and it lasted you for three, four weeks. Nowadays with the drugs, if you're hooked on drugs like I've been, it doesn't last you two hours. The past two years, I'm doing it a lot. I do it because everybody else is doing it, but also to try to escape my problems. And then doing drugs like that, you feel like you're not normal, especially if you're a prostitute. But at least when you're with a trick, it feels like someone wants you.

Last year when I was doing really badly, I got a letter, "Here's a ticket, come claim your property." I am like "Say what?" My aunt that I hardly knew had died and willed me half of her house. I moved down there a thousand miles away and got a job and was doing really well, when I got the telegram that my sister was thrown off a roof. I had tried to get her to move down with me, but she wouldn't leave the City. So I left my job and came back up here. I had planned to go back but my family persuaded me to move back with them and I fell for it, only to leave a week later because the situation, their homophobia, was intolerable. And that was it, back to the streets. Hard to believe, huh, I got a one way ticket out and it lasted eight months.

I don't have any real friends, just a couple of guys I hang out with on the streets. One's upstate in jail, the other I haven't heard from for a few weeks. We used to hang out in the Club House[6] together, hustling, hanging out, smoking crack.

Lately I've been staying some at the Men's Shelter on John's Island. They have substance abuse counselors, job counseling, stuff like that. If you can get over the bridge past the gay bashers in one piece, it's all right. Some guys don't like it because there are so many gays over there, but it's perfect for me. Just like in jail. There's always somebody leaving candy or cigarettes on my bed, wanting to take care of me, be my friend.

I like to help everyone if I can. If I can show a kid where to sleep, send him to the Club House, I do them the favor. Some of my tricks, they take the time to talk to me, they care for me.

They help me out when they're able. Sometimes I go to the Center, I am friendly with some counselors there. I pick up some clothes, a little dinner, then it's time to party. I look so good, you'd never believe I live on the streets. I go to the Sound Factory or Tracks to dance and listen to music, meet people. I see people I know, hang out a while, then back to the Circle.

I'm off the streets now for a few days, staying with my godmother. She treats me like I'm her own son, just like a family. That's something I've missed in my life. Even in my childhood, I never had a real family. I left my aunt's at 13, so mentally I'm filling up that gap that's there.

Rick

My mom died when I was three years old. You know, they didn't even let me go to the funeral. Trying to protect me. From what, from the truth? It was really foul. Everybody just went haywire after she died. My mother was a super provider, the backbone, the strength of the family. She was what kept everybody going. After she passed away nothing got done anymore, there was no more love, no more sharing. When she died it was just like everything just went, "Oh, it's party time, you know, you're not important right now." And my father was with woman after woman and what I felt wasn't important. My feelings didn't count.

When I was little, my father used to drink and do drugs. He don't do drugs no more. He just drinks. He used to sell, reefer as a matter of fact, while he was going to school. I guess that's how he paid the tuition. I remember helping him bag[7] when we were kids. Police came to the house all the time, but he never got arrested. He finished and got his degree and everything.

He used to have his parties and leave me with the aunts and uncles. When I was seven, eight years old, there had to be a twelve year old when it started, we would all go to bed with each other. In the same room, in the same bed. Boy and boy, girl and girl, boy and girl, anybody that got the time. You know, I've always known both so I've always enjoyed both. I thought that was normal. I mean, they came to our house and we went to their house and it was like family togetherness.

There was a great deal of chaos, a great deal of neglect and no supervision whatsoever. We had to do everything ourselves. Cook, clean, iron, get dressed, make my father's coffee, make his girlfriend's coffee. When I could reach the table I was responsible.

My father married this woman finally. She was illiterate. She was a stepmother. You know stepmothers are bitches. She changed him. Twenty-five years younger than him, he needed her to make him feel good. I couldn't live with her, so when I was sixteen, I left home. I couldn't see it. Anyway, he loved me, I know he did. I know he did.

I was tired of him beating me, too. 'Cause he never knew how to be a father. All he ever knew how to do was reprimand. He used to hit me with a belt, you know, he had this leather whip he used on us. It would be like a tradition, you'd have to kneel on the floor and get beat. One time I went out with this Black girl, which is against Puerto Rican mores. You go out with only Puerto Rican. So my stepmother told him I was out with this Black girl. He slapped me up, backhanded me, he was a big strong guy. My face was so deformed and I said, "He is never going to do this to me again, never." That's when I left. The biggest mistake of my life.

So then I was homeless for like the past six years. Well, not 100% homeless, because I stayed here for six months, there for six months, with tricks. My friends said, "You're so handsome and well built, guys would pay to see that." And I was like,

"Where is this place? Take me there!" So starting out, I danced in bars, on stage, in front of a lot of people, men of course, dirty old bucks. It was demoralizing, it was against my upbringing, but I'm not the kind of person to go around robbing somebody. I mean, I could barely hurt a fly. I say that I love life so much I couldn't hurt another human being, but I hurt myself so much.

When my mother died, I started stuffing feelings. I blocked it out. I didn't allow myself to feel the grief of losing her. A big part of me just disappeared. Then I was prostituting and doing what was against my standards, but it didn't matter, my feelings didn't count. When I was dancing, all I had to do was get a hard on and get attention and have people want me. That's all I ever wanted was somebody to want me.

Sometimes I stayed with my brothers. I've had real jobs, clerical work, delivery, Customs. But I was dismissed from the jobs, most times for stealing or getting high. But they never reported me, I never went to jail.

So when I came on the streets, I was dancing to keep my hotel room together. It was thirty bucks a night, but I could make that easy. It was a sleazy motel, but what the heck. The other guys were doing it [dancing] to buy drugs and after three months, I started getting high too and ended up just like them. Doing it to get high. It felt good. Even though I had lots of attention, there was still something missing. And getting high filled the void.

Pretty soon with the drugs, I was hustling pretty heavy. On the streets, all I had to do was just stand out there to get picked up, on account of I'm a good looking guy. Mostly the Wharf or the East Side or occasionally I'd go to bars. See, I'd make some money off a trick and then I'd go to a bar by myself, see somebody sitting down, and ask "Can I buy you a drink?"

So I'd buy them a drink and that was it. A night, two nights, off the streets, $150 for me, they fell for it hook, line, and sinker. I would buy them a drink and they would fall for me big time. I mean, would you pick somebody up who was in the street looking in the garbage can? No. A better class of person would pick me up. It was dinner, the room, the clothes, but most of all, the dope.

I've met some prestigious people. People who took me on business trips and all I had to do was stay in the hotel while they was on their convention and render services when they came back to the hotel. They paid for the plane tickets and everything. As long as the drugs kept coming, I watched TV and took advantage of room service and I thought I was having fun. I thought I was living it up. But actually I was getting more and more lonelier by the minute.

I was in drug treatment for eight months, where I learned I was HIV positive. I left because I didn't know how to handle it. That's when it hit me, you know, "you are positive." "You are positive. You have the AIDS virus, don't you remember?" I would totally block it out, because my mind does that when something hurts. I'm trying to get myself back in treatment. This life sucks. This life is for nobody. I want to be independent, I want to have a good relationship. I have my life, I go to school, I'm gonna go to school.

Tracy

My name is Tracy. I'm very pretty, tall, dark skinned Afro-American woman with almond eyes and a short hair. People they usually think I'm sweet but it don't seem like anything good ever lasted for me.

My mother had me when she was 15. From the time I was born 'til I was about seven, I stayed with my mother and my grandmother. When I was seven, I was molested by my uncle, and my mother put me in foster care for two years. Altogether I was in three foster homes. The first family I stayed with had 13 members in a small apartment. When I was seven, one of the older boys molested me. The next home, it was just me and one of my brothers with the foster parents. They only spoke Spanish, no English. It was lonely there, not being able to talk to no one. The third home was very nice. There was four other sisters, I was in between them age-wise. She was a single mother with her own house. They were very religious. We wanted to stay there, but my father who was in jail found out we was in foster care so he asked his mother that we didn't even know to take us, the Court agreeing to it. Our feelings sure didn't count. So, you know, they moved us again. We were with her for three years. Then my mother come and got us. We didn't really want to go. We wanted to stay with my grandmother. But nobody ever listened to us before. It wasn't no different.

So I stayed with my family somewhat for another three years. My mother wasn't home a lot. She worked during the day. She went to school in the afternoon and went back to work at night. On Saturday, she would take me with her, 'cause she worked all day Saturday. She would take me or my brother, you know, and we'd stay all day at work with her. But then at night, she'd come drop us off and she'd go back out to work. We never saw her. So, I kept the house as far as I cooked, cleaned and watched over my two brothers. They were one and two years younger than me. So we was right behind each other.

My mother and father got problems with drugs. My mother is an alcoholic and my father is an alcoholic and drug addict. My father, he shoots stuff in, and my mother, she just sniffs it. So I guess I came by it easy.

When I was 12 or 13, one of my older friends was turning tricks for money. One night, she had this date and he had a friend, so I went out with them. So we go cop[8] and then we went to her house where she could turn a trick and she was smoking crack, right. I didn't know anything about it, I'd never smoked before. She offered me some and at first I wouldn't try it. But before the night was over, I did try it. Four or five months later, I tried it again and got this acquired taste in my mouth, you know, like I've got to have it.

When my mother was 28, she married a 19 year old guy and she asked me to leave, she thought I was having an affair with him. I wasn't, but my best friend was. My friend had a baby by him the next year. So I left and was on the streets about a year. Then my mother found out she could get in trouble for neglect so she called Children's Services and told them I ran away.

I was too old by then for foster care so they put me in a group home, off and on for four years. Four years now in group homes, the Center, staying with boyfriends, on the streets. I haven't seen my mother in two and a half years.

I have two sons, four and two. My oldest is with my mother, my youngest is in foster care. I haven't seen him in a year and a half.

I was in treatment programs for very short times. The first one, my mother called and told me my son was sick. What it was, she just didn't have a babysitter. I never went back, 'til two years later when I was pregnant again. I went into labor when I was five months and left the program, good bye. My baby was in the hospital for a long time. I used to go see him. I must have stayed there for weeks straight, just sitting there looking at him, wishing there was something I could do for him. He never came home with me. Children's Services took him straight out of the hospital.

I've been in jail several times. Soliciting, possession. An undercover DT[9] snagged me the last time for selling. I have such bad luck. If I pick up a guy in a car it's a cop.

When I started using drugs a lot of guys would just give it to me for nothing, being that I was young and cute, just to have me around, you know. I didn't have to do anything. Then I was stealing little things from around the house, from my mother, not anyone that would hurt me. Around fourteen, that's when I started dating for hire. I knew about it because of reading and my friend turning tricks. And then I was always listening to my mother and her friends. I used to just go out with neighborhood boys, but now I have regular dates or sometimes I stop cars. But I'm scared to pick up just anybody. I got locked up once, getting in somebody's car, another undercover cop. So, I'm cautious about getting into cars or letting someone stop me on the street. If they look a certain way, I don't mess with them. I've been raped. I had one guy pull out a knife and take the money back. When I was hungry, he pulled out a knife and took back the money. I try not to go nowhere, you know, out of the ordinary anymore.

I don't have any friends, except my girlfriend that turned me on and Al that I met that first night. He's about 40 years old. He's my babies' father. The only friends I've got are the dollar bills in my pocket and sometimes you don't even trust yourself with them. Sometimes I think I have a death wish. I never thought I'd live this long. I've tried twice to kill myself, but I can't stand the sight of blood. When I take pills, that don't work either, I just end up in the hospital and get even sicker from that black stuff, charcoal, I think. I feel so hopeless and alone. I like myself, it's just that nobody else does.

What I want, I want to get my kids back. I wanna go somewhere and get treatment and save some money, so they will give me my kids. I love them, I want so much to be a mother to them. But how can you be a good mother when you don't hardly have a mother yourself. I would go to school. I just want to have a place to stay, somebody to talk to.

Paula

There's not a lot to know about me, Katherine. I'm borderline. I'm a prostitute, a heroin addict. I'd just as soon be dead, but I can't even kill myself properly. What else do you want to know?

I grew up in Mississippi. My parents divorced when I was little and my mother remarried—a minister. He used to abuse me. The driver on the church bus molested me when I was young. Then when I was fourteen, I ran away. My parents helped me pack. When I went home two days later, they were gone. It took my social worker a year to find them. I have no family anymore. I need a mother, I need a family. And now I have to go out and work my butt off all night pretending I like it, so I can get a room and a couple of bags of dope. I hate men. Do you know I've been raped four times in the past two years? Four times. Do you blame me for wanting out, for wanting to just go to sleep and not wake up?

I want to get pregnant. I think if I had a baby, someone to love, someone to love me, I could kick.[10] I am trying to get pregnant. I've had a lot of miscarriages, I guess you've seen me flipping out that way a couple of times, but I really want to have a baby.

My girlfriend, she just broke up with me. I was going out with her for a couple of years, staying with her a lot. She's twenty-eight, she has a good job. But she can't handle that she's lesbian. She loves me, but she won't see me. She thinks if she doesn't see me, it will go away. I miss her so much, I just want to die.

I just left the hospital against medical advice. I had pelvic inflammatory disease. They wanted me to stay so I could get IV medicine, but even with Methadone, I couldn't tolerate being in the hospital, I had to get a fix, so I left. But the antibiotics helped, I feel lots better.

My teeth are getting straighter, can you tell? I've had my braces for two years. There is still some more work to do, but I have to save another $1000 to finish. But I've done it all by myself, working on the street, and I can finish. It will just take me a while. I have to, you know, I have to keep up my habit.

I stay in hotels almost all the time. If a trick won't get a room for me, I just keep working 'til I have the money. It's too dangerous on the streets, to let some guy rape you and beat you.

One of my dates, a platonic one, is going to hire me in his business. He is going to help me get a place to live, get me off the streets. Think what it would do for my self-esteem, getting paid to do a real job. To be able to quit working the johns! He's done this before, he helped another girl get off the streets the same way. He introduced her to a client and they're married now. I know I can do it. I can quit using and work and I'll be fine.

Jon

Oh yeah, hi. My name is Jon, no H. You'll have to pardon my accent, I'm not from around here. To introduce myself, I'm tall, kind of thin, with blond hair and blue-green eyes. People say I'm really good looking. Maybe a few years ago, but now I'm not so sure.

I mostly grew up in Sicily with my parents and my younger brother. Then we lived in Paris for a few years. My father being in the military, he was really strict. He used to beat me regularly just for the hell of it. He always used to say, "Look at you. You're such a screw up. You're going to grow up to be a junkie, you know it? You're going to be a junkie and die in the streets." Before I ever smoked a single cigarette he used to tell me this. I joined the military, that being the family vocation, but they disowned me when I deserted. I guess they all hated me. I don't know what I did to make them hate me so much . . .

My brother, he was nine when I left. But he never got beaten like I did. My mother says they're not going to make the same mistakes with him they did with me.

When I was sixteen or so, I forget, I had this friend who started trying to get me high, but it never worked. We smoked reefer and hashish for six months and I couldn't even feel it. So one day he had a friend shoot me up with some dope. Bang. That was it, man. I got high about ten more times, before I got hepatitis. But as soon as I got well, I started using again.

But one thing about me, I never gave drugs to anybody else. Except my ex-wife. She begged and begged me to turn her on, so I finally did. She got hepatitis and never did it again. That's why she left me, because of the drugs. Her daddy bought her a farm in Kentucky and horses when she left me. I was in such pain then I didn't care what happened to me.

I've been here in the U.S. for about four years now. I had always panhandled to get a little money together. It takes a lot of work to get ten dollars panhandling, so I was only using one bag a day, for a long time. One day I was with my wife and two of her gay friends and one of them said, "A nice looking guy like you, you could make money hustling. You could make good money turning tricks. But you'd have to let me check you out, to see that you wouldn't break[11] when you did it." So you know, we did it and it didn't bother me. So I went out that night and got a date and I did break, but he paid me anyway. I got fifty dollars for nothing, and it was like, WOW, so much money after being broke for so long. So I was into it big time. I started hanging out in gay bars, picking up tricks, and I made a lot of money there. I got so bad, I would make some money uptown and run downtown to buy and then run back up and do it again. I wasn't using just a bag a day anymore, that's for sure. I wore myself out til I really looked bad and didn't care about myself and they quit letting me in to the bars 'til I got myself together.

I'm on the Wharf now because I got arrested up on Park Circle twice now for solicitation. I just got out of jail. The cops hate gays and I was so miserable kicking, I thought I couldn't bear it. I'm not getting arrested again, it was too miserable. The cops don't come around down here.

Now I've got a new girlfriend, but lately I'm starting to like guys. What am I going to tell her? She doesn't know I hustle and when she found out I used needles, she just started buying them for me. And she won't let me use rubbers. It's just so confusing, with me starting to like it with guys and not wanting to hurt her or give her anything.

For her I kicked heroin and methadone. And now she's into cocaine?! I go home and she's there spreading lines on the coffee table for me. We bought a house together, but she's a high-priced architect, right? I worked my butt off for two years so I could pay my share. She had dumped me four times and after we bought the house, after I kicked heroin and methadone for her, she dumped me again. I thought she meant it and I was hurting so bad, I just didn't care. So I went back on the street, and you know, I got a bag. Now she comes back again and wants me home every night, laying out cocaine for me. It seems like she's not so keen on me either, jerking me around like I was some kind of yo-yo, sabotaging me getting straight.

Everybody says I seem really smart. But what's the use. I finished the ninth grade, I've done some construction, but I've got nothing to show for it. I feel sometimes like there's nothing for me to do but finish killing myself.

Deborah

Hey, Katrina! What's shaking, bacon? So you want to know how I grew up and got to be here, huh. That could take some time, you know. I grew up by the Market uptown from here, where I lived with my brothers and sisters. Eleven sisters and seven brothers in one apartment to be precise and my parents. Little by little the older ones moved out, 'til there was just ten kids, but then there were the nieces and nephews that kept coming on, so it was always pretty crowded.

On my graduation day for sixth grade, my mother died from some kind of cancer. On my graduation day, I'm telling you. I was eleven years old. Not that things were that good before, but it hurt me so much, the pain got me started hanging out on the street, using drugs, anything to escape that feeling that losing your mother brings. I guess I took it harder than anybody, I'm the only one in my family that uses any drugs. I was using dust, angel dust, that didn't work, so I started messing around with everything else. Twelve years old and I'm using marijuana, cocaine, alcohol. My dad couldn't handle it, so I stayed with a brother, I stayed with a sister. Here and there all over town. A lot of different relatives, different placements, then I just took to staying out on the streets. My family didn't know where I was, they took out a warrant for me. I stay home a little while, then I'm gone again. One time, I started having flashbacks from all the dust and I came to in a psychiatric hospital. Stayed there a month and a half. When I was thirteen, somebody shot some dope into my veins. I liked that a lot, I started hooking to buy it. Then somehow I quit that and just used a lot of alcohol. A lot of alcohol.

I got pregnant at fourteen, had my first baby at fifteen. Sixteen, I started smoking base. Base is crack, crack is cocaine, cocaine is crack. Crack is wack. It got me bad, got me back on the streets. See, the reason kids is homeless is the drugs. Me, I stayed here and there, but the way it is, you stay somewhere, they got house rules. Me, I got my own rules I got to follow. So I never could stay one place for long. The crack be calling me back. And crack, crack will make a rich man poor.

My dad remarried, his wife didn't even know he had us younger kids. So it was a fight to stay with him. She finally accepted me to let me live there, but they made me work all the time, just like *Cinderella*. When I was staying with my brother, his wife accused me of having an affair with him. My own flesh and blood brother with the same parents as I got. I didn't stay there long. Everywhere I go they're putting me out. So it finally came to me living in the Terminal. That's some place. People be hooking and cooking, whoring and making crack. Right there in the Terminal. A bowl, a lighter, cooking up crack, selling it in the stairwells. And me, it don't matter how many locks and bolts and doors there were, I could get through. The police would find me sleeping inside the locked halls or stairwells and kick me around and say, "Yo, Deborah, wake up. I don't know how you keep getting in here." You know they know me real well.

Sixteen, seventeen, more babies, more drugs. I was in jail for a year and a half for cutting off a girl's fingers with a meat cleaver. We was fighting, probably over some guy. Jail's not so bad, a warm place to stay, a bed to sleep on, three squares[12] a day. I got out, I stayed around the Terminal, sometimes overnight at the Center. I been in jail a lot, dealing drugs, soliciting. Now I ain't dealing any, 'cause they catch you with a vial of crack you get one year, automatic. Five vials five years. No thank you.

Right now, I'm back living with my dad. My brother's got all my kids. Four of them now, three boys and a girl. They're good kids too, you know. Deonne, Kishon, Ramone, and Tasha. I don't want no more though. I got more than I can handle already.

I've lost a lot of friends out here on the streets. Some beat up, some drugs or AIDS, some just disappear. One girl, my best friend, bugged out on drugs when she was turning a date, he raped her in the butt, her bleeding and screaming, he beat her to death and she only fifteen years old. I saw that, he wouldn't let me cover for her. It's not good, so many kids dying.

What you'll never guess is that with all the drugs and running around and babies and the craziness of the places I stayed, I still finished high school. Me, Deborah, a high school graduate. I don't know how I did it. A little bit late, but I finished. I guess there's been some few people that was good to me all the time I've been running, that cared about me and took care of me, and hassled me about my life. But the better they treated me, the more I used them. But I didn't know I was using them, it was the crack made me do it. But for all my craziness and problems, I've been blessed, I've had a lot of blessings. My beautiful children, my counselors at the Center. For all the trouble I've had and been in, I've known some good things.

Epilogue

Darryl withdrew from further contact and vanished soon after he heard I was leaving the Center. As of this time, my attempts to locate him have been unsuccessful. After our interviews, Junior was adopted by an extraordinarily supportive gay benefactor, "not a date," he admonished me; the relationship mediated only by Junior's tolerance of structure and intimacy. Junior is working with an AIDS peer counseling program, taking the message of safe sex to his former cohorts about town. He reports he is drug-free and intends to enroll in school shortly. His long-term foster parents have continued to rebuff him in his recent efforts to reconnect with them. He has tentatively renewed relationships with long removed siblings.

Sarah, a minor at the time of our meeting, was interviewed with the consent of her mother. Sarah was remanded to Job Corps after her arrest for dealing. After a brief interlude there, she withdrew once again to the streets, where she presumably remains, lost to follow up.

Louie is believed to be residing in a City-subsidized apartment, continuing his Methadone program. I have seen him infrequently since our interviews, in the Terminal and around the Deuce, apparently high. He no longer visits the Center.

Shortly after Rocco's interview, Rocco was remanded to jail on an outstanding warrant related to robbery charges, where he remains. Rick reentered long-term drug treatment just after this interview and is presumed to be doing well. Center staff pooled resources after her interview to send Tracy to a private treatment program some distance away. She stayed for several months, then relapsed on a short visit to the City, where she found her longed-for oblivion, murdered within a week of arrival. I am told Jon is still on the streets, heroin habit and hustling unabated.

In a truly bizarre twist, Paula became pregnant just after this interview, then received an invitation from her long absent family to return home. At last sighting, she had plane tickets and was on her way home. I interviewed Deborah in the Terminal where I ran into her after my extended absence. She professed she was off the streets and straight. One wants to believe, but her presence there, her continued engagement with street peers which I observed, and her failure to show up the next day for another interview, did not encourage me.

The Streets

In the following sections, I describe the city from my own experiences before and during the research endeavor, from the vantage point of local journalists, and last, from the perspective evinced by my informants. Analysis begins with my first impressions of the field and my learning to see familiar streets in a new way.

The reader should be reminded that the names of people and places are fictitious, excepting my own as it occasionally appears. I would also point out to the reader that quotations derive from three sources—interviews with ten youths, designated by the youth's pseudonyms; the log, designated by the pseudonym of the youth speaking with log citation; and relevant popular literature, so designated.

First Impressions

Aptekar (1988) instructed his readers that the street children of Colombia lived "not just in the streets but in particular streets that had their own history and cultural context" (p. 16). As a long time resident and explorer of the city, I had gained a native's awareness of its streets and neighborhoods. I played pickup basketball in vacant lots and watched performers in the local parks. I mingled with shoppers in the market and mixed with the famous and poseurs in obscure clubs. I rode my bicycle to work in rush hour traffic, assailed by pedestrians and motorists. I was familiar with the subways, buses, angry cabbies, and the hurrying masses.

Acquaintance with the local grocers, florists, and merchants heightened my sense of belonging and neighborhood. I learned in some measure the history of the city and the ebb and flow of its varied populations. This pride of place, then, reassured me as I undertook to learn the streets in a new context, that of street children interacting with the world.

I was disabused of any notion that I inhabited the same world as street youths on my first visit into the field as a researcher and participant observer. Walking down a familiar street at midday, I was struck with a lead pipe by a youthful aggressor. The sense of security I had come to take for granted as I traversed the streets was shattered in a moment and I came to know the uncertainty and unpredictability that obtain when one's dwelling is the streets. It was necessary then to realize that whatever experience I had of the city, the reality for street kids is a different entity altogether.

On subsequent field visits, made in the company of outreach workers, these differences became more apparent. The streets that by day were bustling with commerce gave way at dusk to commuters, diners, theater goers, and revelers. By late night, the streets were largely deserted, the daytimers having retired. Traveling by van from one area to another, I identified pockets of activity or lone individuals idling on a corner, which I came to recognize as prostitution. Particular areas, which I refer to with pseudonyms, Cannery Row, the Wharf, Park Circle, and the Terminal were at midnight and in the early morning hours peopled with derelicts, prostitutes, hustlers, johns, drug dealers, drug users, and occasionally a pair of outreach workers, traveling together for safety. In this environment, I learned that predation and violence were commonplace, death an ever present possibility. This nocturnal place, threatening, hostile, and unknown, was business as usual for street kids.

The Milieu

I have noted in other chapters that street youths commonly frequent isolated areas or public spaces with hidden passages. In the City, isolated often implies undesirable, and such was the case with the varied locations through which I followed street kids. My field notes] describe several impressions:

> We are in a barren area of crumbling brick buildings and stripped, rusted, burned out cars. A fire burns in an abandoned lot where assorted characters are warming their hands and drinking. The food is an unexpected and welcome windfall, I think, considering the excitement it generated. We have exhausted the possibilities now, as the pimps are guarding the girls jealously (we are bad for business) and decide to head back to town. (Log, p. 49.38-48)

> On a side street outside the Terminal, a row of large cardboard boxes and ragged blankets have littered the sidewalk for weeks, the stench of human excreta permeating the air. I am here to look for Sarah. Rocco has seen her earlier smoking crack in one of the boxes, her most recent residence. "Miss Thing, does Katherine know you are out here?" "No! Get out of here! Can't you see I've got a stem?"[13] But the police have cleared out the boxes and the box people and Sarah too has moved on. (Log, p. 72.25-32)

A surge in the body count has seen the Wharf closed off and Cannery Row and Park Circle heavily patrolled. Two or three deaths have occurred on the Circle, with shootings on Cannery Row, and serious attrition on the docks. Arriving at the Wharf, I see a long line of concrete barriers, enclosing the entire length of the parking lot—a good four to six blocks long. The only entry is by a ten foot driveway, which is obstructed now by two or three police cars, several officers on foot or horseback, and wooden barricades. A lone couple strolls down the North end of the lot and a hundred or so kids hang out at the south end, in close proximity to the officers. (Log, p. 95.15-40)

Similar impressions were recorded by a local journalist, speaking to the contrasts of day and night on Cannery Row:

As dusk falls, the neighborhood becomes the domain of dozens of drug-addicted men in drag, looking for an invitation to one of the slow moving cars, vans and limousines—many with Jersey plates—that prowl the street. In the shadows, near the loading docks, pimps and dealers oversee the nocturnal meat market . . . The brisk trade begins to fade by early morning. The meat packers arrive, the Yuppies dress for work, and daylight makes prostitution a more tricky proposition. There are rubbers of all colors on the sidewalk. Green, lavender, pink—and about 50 crack vials. (Nolan, 1990, p. 13)

The Wharf was formerly a prosperous shipping port. Bounded on the North by the City's sanitation facilities, the area is characterized by long dilapidated piers that jutted out into the broad river. Rotting and missing planks made walking hazardous. The City had erected fences to thwart would-be trespassers, to little effect. The Wharf paralleled a neighborhood in transition, where seedy hotels, disreputable bars, and decaying buildings were intermingled with exclusive cooperative housing and more refined businesses.

Park Circle was an area four blocks square, located in a more rarified part of the City. Art galleries, upscale boutiques, exclusive restaurants, and casually elegant bars lined the quiet sidewalks and expensive high rise apartment buildings abutted tasteful brownstones. Residents, business people, and sightseers to this district possessed an aura of confidence and prosperity, in marked contrast to pedestrians I observed in other locations.

The Alley differed from the Wharf, the Cannery, and the Circle in that it was located in a quiet residential area at some distance from Downtown. Older brick houses and neatly trimmed lawns imparted a sense of propriety and permanence to the area, an improbable setting for the commerce it quartered.

These passages are cited at length to communicate not only the desolate physical surroundings which prevailed, but the tension that is manifest in the streets after dark. The silence that was sometimes observed, as in Overlook, seemed charged and more than once, the stillness signaled the aftermath of shootings or other casualties.

The nocturnal rhythms street youths follow are implicit in the preceding paragraphs. The self-imposed spatial and temporal isolation street kids evince perpetuates their sense of separation, alienation, and invisibility. This phenomenon is discussed in greater detail in Relationships with the Mainstream.

Street Kids' Perspectives of The Streets

I learned as I approached youths on the streets and questioned them that their perspectives of the streets were far broader than what I or most journalists had admitted. The streets, populated by thousands of estranged youths, represented to them a throbbing, vital center of activity, socialization, and commerce, expressed in the themes, "The streets are my refuge—where life is happening" and "The streets give me what I need."

> It was a real life out there because at that time I was going to the Wharf and hanging out in the streets and vogueing and you know, that's all anybody knew and going to balls and staying out 'til 5:00 in the morning. (Rocco, p. 6.14-19)

> I was hanging out on the street corner dealing drugs (Louie, p. 6.25). I was making good money (Louie, p. 7.13). I was on the streets, hustling my butt off. (Louie, p. 18.14-15)

> The streets is turning dollars. If you ever go out with a guy for five dollars, you must be out of your head or on drugs (Sarah, p. 2.1-3). A typical day on the streets I'll be on the Deuce making money. (Sarah, p. 20.15)

Education, danger, deprivation, distrust, fear, intrigue, excitement, fun, and loneliness describe the experiences various youths recounted of the streets. Rocco spoke of the learning he had gained on the streets:

If maybe my mother had stuck it out we could have had everything and could have been 'normal kids.' Instead I had to experience the streets, which I don't regret, because I've learned a lot. (Rocco, p. 12.17-21)

Sarah noted the treachery and her distrust of the streets:

The streets are terrible, you know (Sarah, p. 28.22). Sidewalks talk and you'd better watch what you do and what you say. I mean, sidewalks talk, that means everybody's out to get you (Sarah, p. 29.2-9). You've got to know who to trust and who not to trust. Cause sidewalks talk. (Sarah, p. 30.2-3)

Darryl and Tracy described the danger and deprivation:

Very scary (Darryl, p. 8.18). I'm afraid someone's going to come up and shoot me or kill me, you know, it's rough, it's very rough (Darryl, p. 9.1-2). One night I slept on the train and I had no jacket and it was snowing out and I was freezing to death and I was very very sick and no one wouldn't help me (Darryl, p. 10.12-15). One day I was starving so bad I couldn't get no money so I had to dig in the garbage can to get something to eat, a piece of trash, I remember. (Darryl, p. 10.22 and p.11.1-3)

I've been raped. I've had one guy pull out a knife and take the money back. When I was hungry, one of my dates when I was hungry, he pulled out a knife and took the money back. (Tracy, p. 26.14-19)

Louie and Junior, although recognizing the street's dangers, nevertheless remained enamored of the intrigue of street life.

The streets are so funny. It's not a game out there. Lots of them think its a game. It's not a game. It's a jungle out there, it's not a game, it is a game. It's a very dangerous game, I'll tell you that (Louie, p. 29.1-6). It's not one to get involved in, because once you get involved, it's hard as hell to get uninvolved. (Louie, p. 29.8-11)

The streets mean trouble. I don't know, it's exciting somewhat. It can be very exciting (Junior, p. 9.7-8). And dangerous. Just recently, in the past year, three people have been killed in the back of the Alley (Junior, p. 14.1-3). Sometimes it can be real fun just being out there. That cat and mouse game you play with the cops. (Junior, p. 27.3-5)

Goldsmith (1993) remarked, "on the street, danger is omnipresent. If a prostitute disappears, no one asks any questions; many prostitute deaths go unnoted" (p. 79). Solotaroff (1990) inquired of a street kid about the whispered rumors of death on the docks, to which the youth replied, "All these motherfuckers they've been pulling out of the river, what do you think, they fell off their yacht?" (p. 36). These citations were, incidentally, the only references I found to the many deaths that summer, deaths which were verified by police, outreach workers, kids, and local residents.

Several investigators have noted the addictive quality of streetlife (Visano, 1991; Weisberg, 1985; C. Williams, 1993). As informant Cassie remarked to Sereny (1985), "I guess its like an addiction. I just get so used to going out there. It's a good way to stop yourself from thinking" (p. 73).

Rick cited the uncertainty and aimlessness of street life:

> Very unpredictable. Very unstable. Very scary. Scary like, everything's unpredictable. I hate to be like that. I hate not to know. Very worriful, I mean. Like an endless blank. No meaning, no purpose, no goal. (Rick, p. 12.11-18)

The latter passages cohere particularly with the analyses of two other researchers. "The street," according to Hartman et al. (1987), is "an open environment that is unprotective, enticing, and exploitative" (p. 294). Aptekar (1988) described "the streets" as "a nearly archetypal place of anonymity, where family name had no meaning, where family connections were worthless, but where one's personal abilities to get the job done were paramount to survival" (p. 155). The addiction to the streets which Junior and Louie described, the excitement and danger, represent a phenomenon of vital importance as will be demonstrated.

Notes

1. A highly refined form of crack.

3. An allusion to cocaine.

4. A bundle is a unit of crack equivalent to a market value of $1,000.

5. See Pumps and Pearls, p. 84, 115, 154, 158, 166, 173.

6. See Junior and Group Life, p. 152.

7. To package marijuana.

8. To procure or purchase illicit drugs.

9. Vernacular for detective.

10. Vernacular for drug withdrawal.

11. To "freak out" or lose control.

12. Meals.

13. Vernacular for crack pipe.

V

Facets of Life:
Core Categories and Themes

Introduction

As I analyzed the data, categories and themes coalesced around two principal dimensions, those of the youths' lived experiences and their interior perceptions and beliefs. In the present chapter I have identified *Facets of Life* common to many or all of the youths' experiences in growing up, in moving onto the streets, and in living and surviving on the streets. *Facets of Life* addresses the central research question about the lived experiences of the youths.

The youths' experiences of others were instrumental in defining the boundaries of their worlds. Relationships with family, progeny, friends, helping professionals, mainstream society, the Law, and local residents are explicated in succeeding sections and refer to the research subquestion about the social contacts of the youths. Prostitution, getting high, survival strategies, and solitary or group life, dominant aspects of street experience for my informants, are accorded separate sections. Because categories and themes were drawn from the same raw material as the previous vignettes, some repetition is apparent.

Family Then and Now

Past Family Experience

As I sought to understand the realities of youths' experiences of the streets it seemed relevant to inquire about their backgrounds, as well as present family relationships. The events and elements of Rocco's background, summarized below, were common to many of the youths I studied.

Born to a working class, two parent family, Rocco's mother abandoned the household when he was three years old. His father, unable to manage the family, surrendered the children to various relatives, who shuttled them here and there, from the West Coast to Puerto Rico. He was sexually abused by an older cousin from the age of nine to twelve. Rocco left home at twelve, feeling rejected by his [extended] family for his gay identification. On the streets, he became involved in prostitution and drug use. Two years ago, Rocco's father killed himself, still unable to comprehend his wife's desertion. Rocco's sister, who had run away as well, was killed recently when acquaintances threw her from a roof, her murder a graphic reading of the *rockhouse tossup* script.[1]

These historical elements of loss, neglect, and abuse, are represented in several related themes: "I've lost so much, it's hard to risk getting close to someone," "I've been abused and neglected so much, that's all I expect from people," and "I've been exploited—molested, raped, and sexually abused—all my life, mostly by the people who were supposed to take care of me. It's all I've ever known." I have illustrated these themes below with selected summations and passages from the data.

Many youths recounted litanies of overwhelming losses coupled with abandonment and rejection, illustrated by the theme, "I've lost so much, it's hard to risk getting close to someone." As noted above, Rocco was deserted by his mother, rejected by his aunt's family, and then lost his father and sister to violent deaths. Louie's biologic parents were killed in a plane crash when Louie was an infant, then his adoptive parents scapegoated and rejected him. Jon was maligned, rejected, then disowned by his parents. Junior's mother was disabled by mental illness just after his birth and shortly thereafter, his father abandoned him. At thirteen, he was rejected by his foster parents. Rick described the changes in his family which followed his mother's death in this passage:

> My mom died when I was three (Rick, p. 3.7). She was like a super provider. She was the backbone of the family. She was what kept everything going. After she passed away, nothing got done, there was no more love, no more sharing. (Rick, p. 5.6-11)

Deborah described the loss of her mother, rejection by family, and subsequently, the loss of friends to violence, drugs, and AIDS.

The extreme loss and rejection my informants reported were consonant with findings of other researchers (Adams et al., 1985; Beyer, 1974; Englander, 1984; Hartman et al., 1987; Kufeldt & Nimmo, 1987; V. Price, 1989; Saltonstall, 1984; Stiffman, 1989). Roberts (1982a) and Speck, Ginther, and Helton (1988) in particular noted higher incidences of stressful life events in first time runaways and recidivist runaways than in their nonrunaway peers.

As I listened to youths describing their past experiences, I was impressed that some spoke with tears, some with disbelief, and still others with resignation. It was evident that for each of the speakers, the past was still very much part of the present, enduring in their self-perceptions and expectations. I have called this theme "I've been abused and neglected so much, that's all I expect from people."

I remember when I was small, my dad used to beat up my mom and drink. I remember when he used to hang me out the window and threaten to drop me. Once, he did. What happened was that when the police came, he would use me as his shield to make sure they wouldn't shoot him. (Darryl, p. 7.16-23)

My house was a battlefield (Sarah, p.7.21). You could never have like a decent conversation in there. Somebody arguing or picking on somebody. Criticizing me especially (Sarah, p. 8.1-8). My mother used to put me inside the shower buck naked and whip me with an extension cord, hit me with the heel of a high-heeled shoe (Sarah, p.8.14-17). Why was she always careful to hit me so much? It got to where I wouldn't cry after three hours of getting beat and she wouldn't stop 'til I got a tear come from my eye. (Sarah, p. 9.7-11)

V. Price (1989) stated that "Street youths tend to come from families characterized by a high degree of discord and dysfunction" (p. 77). Heightened levels of family conflict such as that described above were confirmed by other researchers (Adams et al., 1985; Beyer, 1974; Crystal, 1986; Goldmeier & Dean, 1973; Loeb, Burke, & Boglarsky, 1986; Roberts, 1982a, 1982b; Saltonstall, 1984; Spillane-Grieco, 1984; Wolk & Brandon, 1977) as well.

Physical abuse of the runaway was also commonly reported (Cavaiola & Schiff, 1988; Hartman et al., 1987; Janus et al., 1987; V. Price, 1989; Saltonstall, 1984; Stiffman, 1989; A. Williams, 1977). Such abuse ranged from harsh or undeserved punishment (Goldmeier & Dean, 1973) to being kicked, bitten, hit with fist or other object, or assault with a knife or gun (Gelles, cited in Farber et al., 1984). Powers et al. (1988) specified telephones, extension cords, chains, belt buckles, and broom sticks as some of the objects with which youths were beaten.

Rick, Tracy, and Darryl specified that one or both parents used alcohol or drugs, a practice that seemed to exacerbate the existing chaos. V. Price (1989), Roberts (1982a, 1982b), Saltonstall (1984), Shaffer and Caton (1984), and A. Williams (1977) found that substance abuse was common among the parents of their informants.

A pattern of sexual abuse expressed in the theme, "I've been exploited—molested, raped, and sexually abused—all my life, mostly by the people who were supposed to take care of me. It's all I've ever known," was commonly evinced by my informants. Rick, growing up with an extended family, reported that an older cousin initiated diffuse sexual relations among his siblings and cousins. Paula and Sarah were molested by their step-fathers, Rocco by his cousin, Angela by multiple adult male relatives, Louie by his father, Teddy by his uncles, and Bo by his step-mother. Teddy gave this account: "Let me put it this way. I grew up in Indiana with some very weird and bizarre relatives. Like, one of my uncles used to lock me up and then let me out and urinate on me" (Teddy, Log, p. 76.24-28).

Consistent with my observations, many researchers (Cavaiola & Schiff, 1988; Covenant House New Jersey, 1990a; Hartman et al., 1987; Office of the Inspector General, 1983; Powers et al., 1988; V. Price, 1989; Saltonstall, 1984; Stiffman, 1989; A. Williams, 1977) and journalists (Hersch, 1988; Solotaroff, 1990) have noted the prevalence of sexual abuse among runaway youths. Silbert and Pines (1983) studied the incidence of prior sexual abuse among 200 current and former street prostitutes. A preponderance of the active prostitutes were under twenty-one years of age. Sixty percent of subjects reported histories of sexual abuse, of whom 17% ran away as a consequence of the abuse. Fifty-nine percent of perpetrators were relatives, 31% friends or acquaintances, and 10% strangers. Silbert and Pines indicated that such sexual abuse included exploitation, which implied manipulation or coercion by a partner, incest, which might involve a parent, sibling or other family member, and rape. Abuse assumed the range of sexual experience, including fondling, genital, anal, and oral intercourse, penetration of vagina or anus with an object, and photographing of these activities (Silbert & Pines). Evidence that the youths' past experiences reverberated in their present lifestyles, suggested by the themes elaborated above, is presented in a later discussion of the youths' existing relationships.

Present Family Experience

My informants reported three patterns of present family relationships: contact with reconciliation, contact with conflict, and no contact. Those reporting conflict cited their families' disappointment and ire about the street kids' lifestyles. Nevertheless, these families evidenced a willingness to reengage with the youths. Chris manifested the first pattern, expressed in the theme "I'm getting along with my family better now":

> I was in jail, all I could think about was if my mom still liked me, whether she sent me anything (Chris, Log, p. 21.14-17). So I'm back at home now, I'm getting along OK with my parents. It's like I disappointed them all I could. I'm gay, I'm a male prostitute, I'm a thief. (Chris, Log, p. 21.22-28)

Talitha, an attractive young transvestite, summarized his mother's ambivalence toward him or perhaps his own fear of abandonment:

I go to see my mother all the time and my mother says to me, 'Look at you child, you're always coming in here to visit me.' Well, one day you are going to show up and I'm not going to be here. But I'll be in the hall waiting, just like always! (Talitha, Log, p. 69.53-54 & p. 70.1-5)

Rocco exhibited the pattern expressed in the theme, "We make up, then we break up," noting the persistence of conflict upon renewed contact with his family:

Before I even left Florida, my family had convinced me that everything was going to be alright. You know that happened before. This isn't a new thing here. And I once again fell for it and came back to their house, only to leave a week later because the situation was unbearable (Rocco, p. 30.3-10). Again they were homophobic. They still are. And the tension in the air was just too much. (Rocco, p. 30.23-26)

Most youths, however, denied any contact with their families, a pattern articulated in the theme "I don't have any family." Junior said that he had tried to stay in contact with his favored foster parents, "but due to my lifestyle, they don't want to speak to me any longer" (Junior, p. 3.7-8). Researchers at the University of Minnesota (cited in "Parent talk," 1991) supported Rocco's and Junior's stories, indicating that one quarter of all homeless youths were ejected from their homes because of their sexual orientation.[2] Sarah, Paula, Jon, and Tina, on the streets for one to six years, reported that their families had utterly abandoned them, disappearing without a trace, a phenomenon noted by other researchers (Feitel et al., 1992; Murphy & Rosenbaum, 1992). Of her lost parents, Tina remarked, "They're my ghost family!" (Deborah, audiotape). Louie, traumatized by a sadistic and withholding father, expressed tremendous anger toward his parents.

It's been five years since I've seen them. Five years since I've seen my [adoptive] parents. I never want to see them again in my life. I don't care if they're dead or alive (Louie, p. 14.26-29). I don't want to see them again, I don't even want to know about it. I sleep perfect without knowing about 'em. You know what I mean, I could care less about them. They never gave me nothing, so what do I care? (Louie, p. 15.1-6)

Three youths, now estranged from their families, told me of deliberate sabotage inflicted by their families. Tracy, seeking sobriety in a drug treatment residence, was called home because her child was seriously ill. Upon leaving treatment, she discovered that her mother had just wanted a babysitter. Two years passed before she returned to treatment. Jon was told by his father, "Look at you. You're such a screw-up. You're going to grow up to be a junkie, you know it? You're going to be a junkie and die in the streets" (Jon, Log, p. 64.40-43).[3] His tentative efforts to withdraw were now frustrated by his girlfriend, who arranged lines of cocaine on her coffee table for him.

Scapegoating and negative labeling like that Jon's father projected were associated with runaway episodes by several researchers (Beyer, 1974; V. Price, 1989; Rothman & David, 1985; Saltonstall, 1984; Spillane-Grieco, 1984). Powers et al. (1988) identified other forms of emotional maltreatment as well, which included extreme verbal abuse, name calling, derogatory remarks, constant yelling, and blaming. Overt rejection and abandonment of youths were noted by Adams et al. (1985), Hartman et al. (1987), Kufeldt and Nimmo (1987), V. Price (1989), and Saltonstall (1984).

My informants' stories supported the extraordinary and profound abuse, chaos, repeated losses, and series of living arrangements and institutionalization reported by other researchers, cited in previous sections. The Institute of Medicine (1989), which studied mental illness in the young, labelled this constellation of maltreatment and disadvantages "persistent psychosocial adversity," and linked it to subsequent emotional disturbances, developmental impairments, and disrupted social adjustment.

Getting to the Streets

The present respondents reported prolonged neglect prior to their departures, articulated in the theme "I was always on my own." Various youths expressed this sense of virtual abandonment: "My mom? She never cared about me. I've been on the streets since I was nine" (Ruthie, Log, p. 7.25-27). "They didn't take care of me, I did everything" (Louie, p. 4.24). "I feel there was a great deal of chaos, there was a great deal of neglect and no supervision whatsoever" (Rick, p. 26.16-18). My informants, growing up in an atmosphere of indifference, conflict, and unpredictability, were socialized to the streets by default:

> We had to do everything ourselves. Cook, clean, iron, get dressed, make my father's coffee, make his girlfriend's coffee (Rick, p. 27.9-12). When I could reach the table I was responsible. (Rick, p. 27.17-18)

> My mother wasn't home a lot (Tracy, p. 2.11). She worked during the day. She went to school in the afternoon and went back to work at night. On Saturday, she would take me with her 'cause she worked all day Saturday. . . Then at night she would drop us off and she'd go back out to work. We never saw her. So, I kept the house as far as I cooked, cleaned, and watched over my two brothers. (Tracy, p. 2.15-25)

Additional evidence for this theme was seen in the large numbers of younger adolescents I observed—at the Wharf, Park Circle, and Cannery Row, youths as young as ten or twelve interacted casually with older kids and tricks until the early hours of morning. Powers et al. (1988) and Saltonstall (1984) defined neglect as typically involving inadequate guardianship, abandonment, lack of supervision, or not providing adequate food, clothing, and medical care, findings confirmed by other investigators (Covenant House New Jersey, 1990a; Hartman et al., 1987; V. Price, 1989). The parental role reversal reflected in this theme was affirmed by Berger (1989), Mirkin et al. (1984), V. Price (1989), and Saltonstall (1984).

Kennedy et al. (1990) speculated that more children and youths will lose home and family as crack use and HIV illness proliferate, phenomena that have already been observed in many larger cities (Yancey, 1992). Over 5,000 children were orphaned by AIDS in 1991 alone, most of whom were "poor, Black or Hispanic, and living in communities least equipped to care for them" ("Number of AIDS orphans grows," 1992).

Aptekar (1988) observed that although a few street children had been neglected or abused, many poor children of Colombia were often purposefully socialized to early independence. Children so raised moved to the streets first by daytime exploration and with progressively longer absences attained a high degree of self-sufficiency. The children who chose the streets, in fact, fared better in most respects than siblings who remained at home. Aptekar indicated that this "method of childrearing is deliberate and helpful in training children to be independent and self-assured in an 'economic subculture of urban poverty' " (p. 182).

I've Experienced Chaos in the Home, Chaos in the Group Home

I have chosen to include the minority theme, "I've never had a real home," with tentative support because so many of my informants, now considered deviant, had experienced foster care during their formative years. Tracy, Rocco, Darryl, Angel, and Junior reported multiple kinship, foster, and group homes or institutions prior to leaving the setting for the streets. This theme finds support in earlier research by Allen, Bonner, and Greenan (1988), Barden (1991), and Feitel et al. (1992), who indicated that foster care graduates were vastly over represented among the homeless.

Angela, Tracy, and Rocco told me that they had been molested in foster homes. Sarah, commenting on the lack of supervision within a group home she visited, stated that she left the home after a brief introductory visit "because you could get drunk in the home now" (Sarah, p. 33.10-11). I also include salient comments by minor informant Linda without other descriptive data. Linda told us after running from her group home:

> I run away from my group home. I run away from it all the time. You can do anything there (Linda, Log, p. 72.20-23). People can do anything there. They don't care. [You feel you need more structure?] Yeah, more rules, making kids follow the rules. (Linda, Log, p. 73.35-38)

De'Ath and Newman (1987) note that authorities are often reluctant

> to acknowledge that the youngster may have a valid perception of how arrangements could be different and

a lack of willingness to openly discuss an alternative placement. . . and negotiate the possibilities. (p.16) [4]

Tracy noted that on two occasions, the court uprooted her from stable kinship and foster homes against her own desire to stay:

> My father was in jail and he heard we was in foster care, so he asked his mother to send for us. We wanted to stay there. My grandmother, we didn't even know my grandmother, my father's mother. We didn't even know she existed, til she came along. And as to the court, we ain't got nothing to things that count. So they took us. You know, they moved us again. (Tracy, p. 1, 27-28, 30-32; p. 2, 1-4, p. 4, 25-30)

Although my research provides limited evidence in this regard, other sources have documented well the adverse effects of surrogate placements on vulnerable children (Institute of Medicine, 1989; Rutter, 1981). Hartman et al. (1987), and others (Kennedy et al., 1990; Kufeldt & Nimmo, 1987; Wilkinson, 1987) noted the high frequency with which youths fled institutional care, an observation which led them to charge society "with systemic neglect and abuse" (p. 531) of adolescents. Solotaroff (1990) concurred in this judgment, referring to the City's foster care system as a "sprawling pathology factory" (p. 34).

Many researchers have documented "a disruption in the capacity to form warm and lasting relationships" (Goldfarb, 1955, cited in Rutter, 1972, p. 102) among youths experiencing early or prolonged institutionalization (Carlson, Cicchetti, Barnett, & Braunwald, 1989; Crittenden, 1988). Bender and Yarnell (1941), Bowlby (1966), Goldfarb, (1943, cited in Rutter, 1972), Rutter (1972; 1981), and Theis (cited in Prugh & Harlow, 1966), noted diminished intellect and the development of later antisocial behavior as well in many children so raised. Researchers have speculated that multiple mothering occurring in "a succession of unsatisfactory and unstable arrangements" (Moore, cited in Rutter, 1972), such as those experienced by my informants, are associated with unfavorable cognitive and emotional effects. Diminished adult-child interaction (Rheingold, cited in Rutter, 1972), the inflexibility of institutional care (Provence & Lipton, cited in Rutter, 1972), and lack of communication and responsiveness to the children's needs (David & Appell, cited in Rutter, 1972) were said to characterize such placements. That some of these youths should ultimately turn to the streets would appear a natural consequence of their accumulated injuries.

On My Own

Wounded by sustained neglect and abuse, my informants responded by early separation from the family. The theme of early self-sufficiency, "I was always on my own," was replaced in the here and now by "I can make it on my own," as my informants projected a continued sense of independence and resignation on the streets. This attitude, I believe, betrayed a deeper fear of abandonment or rejection:

> I don't expect nothing from nobody. I don't ask nobody for nothing. I don't. I don't ask nobody for nothing. Everybody asks me for something, but I don't ask nobody for nothing. I don't, like, you know, it's not my style. (Louie, p. 36.10-15)

> When people hand me money sometimes out of the clear blue sky, I give it back to them. Because it hurts me to take money from a person, for me to ask. (Darryl, p. 21.19-22)

Similarly, V. Price (1989) observed that youths developed a "street bravado of toughness to mask the loneliness within" (p. 87).

Relationships

Parenting

Disrupted family relationships were seen to exist beyond the youths' families of origin. Several informants disclosed the existence of progeny to me, expressing a theme I have articulated as "I have done one thing well." Although these parents expressed pride and interest in their offspring, rarely did they assume a tangible presence in the lives of their children:

> I have two sons, they're four and two. My oldest child is with my mother. I haven't seen either of them in two and a half years (Tracy, p. 9.17-23, p. 10.1-2). My youngest is in foster care and I haven't seen him in a year and a half (Tracy, p. 10.4-5). My younger son was born at five months (Tracy, p. 11.10), he never came home with me. They took him from the hospital (Tracy, p.11.28-29). I used to go see him. I think I stayed there for weeks straight, just sitting there looking at him. Wishing I could do something for him. (Tracy, p. 12.10-15)

> My girlfriend, she's the one that's got my daughter (Louie, p. 39.24), she's two and a half years old (Louie, p. 40.1, 6, 15). She's beautiful, I mean she's really beautiful. I see her and her mom all the time, we just don't live together. But you know now, I have a healthy daughter. (Louie, p. 41.9-10)

Offspring of my male informants most often lived with their domiciled mothers. The children of my female informants were in kinship or foster homes, having been abandoned by the mother or removed by protective services because of the mother's neglect or drug use, in a self-perpetuating cycle, an observation supported by other researchers (Yancey, 1992).

In other salient work, Pennbridge, MacKenzie, and Swofford (1991) conducted a comparison study of domiciled and homeless pregnant adolescents and reported that the homeless youths manifested higher incidences of depression, suicide attempts, and previous physical and sexual abuse than their domiciled peers. Substance abuse, multiple sexual partners, STD's, and other serious medical disorders compounded the risks that poor nutrition, diminished social supports, and discontinuity of care imposed on the homeless adolescent relative to her pregnancy.

Deisher, Litchfield, and Hope (1991) identified identical risks among a group of pregnant adolescents engaging in prostitution. Over half of the adolescents were multiparous, and most reported use of alcohol, cocaine, cigarettes, and/or marijuana just prior to delivery. Forty-four percent of subjects had a least one sexually transmitted disease at delivery. Other complications of the antepartum and parturition included pregnancy induced hypertension, amnionitis, precipitous delivery, premature rupture of membranes, and placental abruption. A high incidence of perinatal complications coincided with maternal morbidity, and included preterm and premature births, intrauterine death, small or large gestational age, decreased head circumference, respiratory distress, drug related symptomatology, meconium staining, increased muscle tone, congenital syphilis, and feeding problems.

Rich (1990) studied bonding in a group of 17 maternal-infant dyads who were residing in a residential program for homeless pregnant and parenting adolescents and their infants. The mothers, 12 of whom were runaways or throw-aways, were domiciled and stabilized at the time of the study; none were currently using drugs or alcohol. The homeless parenting adolescents performed remarkably well on scored observations, in a manner comparable to a larger sample of older well-educated, affluent, married mothers. Rich attributed the high scores of the adolescent mothers to their expressed desire to be capable mothers, the program's educational emphasis on parenting, the role modeling effected by nursery staff, and the mothers' previous child care experience. While Rich's respondents were not representative of more distressed street youths, her study offers strong support for more aggressive intervention with homeless pregnant adolescents.

That street youths, uniformly assumed to be sexually active, are in fact often pregnant or parents is an observation sustained in the literature (Covenant House New Jersey, 1990c; Crystal, 1986; Feitel et al., 1992; Goldsmith, 1993; Kennedy et al., 1990; Manov & Lowther, 1983; M.J. Robertson, 1989; Rotheram-Borus et al., 1992). Kennedy (personal communication, August 27, 1992) observed that the Center had seen three related generations of street kids during its twenty year existence. Crack cocaine and *ice*,[5] substances commonly used by my informants, have often been reported to have a powerful negative effect on parenting (Balshem et al., 1992; Garrett, 1990; Lecayo, 1989; Yancy, 1992), an impression my clinical and research experience supported, my research was insufficient to draw conclusions with respect to this issue.

Friends and Family

Three distinct but overlapping patterns were discerned regarding friendships among street kids. These are expressed in the themes, "I don't have any friends," "We are family," and "I help others and they help me." The first pattern, represented in the theme, "I don't have any friends," reflected a sense of abject loneliness and aloneness, even a fear of being cared for:

> I don't have any friends. I don't have enough time to make friends (Darryl, p. 9.4-5). Every time someone cares I try to push them away a little bit (Darryl, p. 21.5-6). I don't know what love is. I've never been loved before so that's why I push people away. (Darryl, p.21.9-11)

> Actually, most of us don't get along until it's time to go to sleep. I, uh, none of us had nothing to say to each other unless it's "Move over," or "Can I borrow your blanket," or "This enough space for us." You know, other than that, we don't have nothing to say to each other. (Tracy, p. 15.9-16)

> [Do you have any friends on the streets?] No, my friends are the dollar bills that I keep in my pocket. And sometimes you don't even trust yourself with the dollars in your pocket. You can't. (Tracy, p. 25.17-21)

> I don't have any friends. I have no friends that I know of in the streets. I don't consider anybody out there a friend. Because when the going gets tough, they get going, very easily. Everybody out there, when you have money, they are your friends. When you have drugs, they're your friend, or alcohol or cigarettes, cigarettes especially, if they don't have any money,

they're going "Do you have a cigarette?" They will try to get over on you any second that they can. (Junior, p. 22.18-22 and p. 23.1-11)

Simon et al. (1992) indicated that "most of their subjects responded that they have no friends" (p. 42). Saltonstall (1984) noted the capricious nature of street friendships in her study, indicating that abuse and exploitation were common. V. Price (1989) and Saltonstall identified the theme of loneliness among street children in their samples as well.

The converse of this pattern is expressed in the theme, "We are family." Youths manifesting this pattern reported that they had a few "close friends," and called one another "brothers and sisters" by mutual agreement. The reality, however, often belied their words:

> Close friends, close friends, I've really not had no friends on the streets, but, but, there's just one, yes, I'm very, very close to. And I still am. He's away in jail. (Rocco, p. 35.4-10) He told me "I love you cause you're like my brother," and "you are my brother." And from then on, we started calling each other brothers, but him is basically the only one I've ever gotten close to, and then there was another one recently, I don't know what the hell's wrong with him, he hasn't called me in weeks (Rocco, p. 35.22-31). He's basically a friend too. A very close friend. (Rocco, p. 36.22-23)

> My friends on the street, we call each other brothers and sisters. I've been friends with Rhonda since I was on the streets (Sarah, p. 15.16-22). The friends that I have, they cool. The friends that you know are doing better than you expect, they're out to get you. So you've got to know who to trust and who not to trust. Cause sidewalks talk. (Sarah, p. 30.1-3)

Rocco reminisced about the sense of belonging he found in the street scene:

> The gay pier scene. You go to the pier and it's like, you know, hanging out. On the Wharf, down Thomas Street at the end. It was like security, you know, hey I'm here (Rocco, p. 8.14-20). It was like my family away from home. My gay family. (Rocco, p. 9.1-4)

Liebow (1967) observed the fluidity of personal relationships which was evident among the street corner men of *Talley's Corner*:

> Lacking depth in both past and present, friendship is easily uprooted by the tug of economic or psychological self-interest or by external forces acting against it. . . . It is as if friendship is an artifact of desire, a wish relationship, a private agreement between two people to act 'as if,' rather than a real relationship between persons. (p. 206-207)

Aptekar (1988) contrasted the intimate and enduring relationships or chumships street children in Colombia developed with the casual and fleeting friendships he observed among North American street youths. He believed that such chumships were salubrious and contributed to the relative emotional intactness of his informants.

The third pattern is that evinced by a few youths and consists of helping behaviors offered to one's friends. I have treated this pattern as a subcategory, for reasons that will become clear.

Helping and Being Helped

The theme "I help others and they help me" is reflected to a degree in the present study. For Sarah, this took the form of sharing her possessions: "You all, like, we all share" (Sarah, p. 16.11). Rocco and Louie expressed similar feelings:

> I like to help, I like to help everyone I can. In any way that I can, I mean, that's always been me, you know, in any way that I can. Even like the Club House, you know, I'd see a kid sleeping on a doorstep. It's not much, but it's away from everybody. "Go to the Club House. It's away." People you see on the doorstep, I always did things like that. (Rocco, p. 36.29-35)

> I don't hang out with people (Louie, p. 35.10). There's a few friends, like two, two or three (Louie, p. 35.14-15). A couple of kids on the street. They're in trouble, they need something, need a place to stay, I'll give 'em a place. If they need food, need a few dollars, I'll give 'em a few dollars. You know what I mean? (Louie, p. 36.3-6). Whenever I need something, if I need it, they got it, they'll give it to me. (Louie, p. 36.8-9)

Aptekar (1988) and Liebow (1967) identified a common theme of helping and being helped in their respective studies. Liebow stated "In ways such as these [loaning money, sharing goods] each person plays an important part in helping and being helped by those in his personal network" (p. 175). Aptekar indicated that within the *gallada*, the older youths or *jovenes*, assumed the role of elder statesmen or officers, and took responsibility for aiding the enlisted, or younger children. The relationship also provided the *jovenes* with an acceptable way to express affection and concern to the younger children. This "protective device of helping and being helped" enhanced the confidence and competence of both parties.

Wilkinson's (1987) explanation for the relationships street kids formed with one another spoke to the process of socialization to family, peers, and culture. Drawing on Berger and Luckmann (cited in Wilkinson, 1987), Wilkinson indicated that by adopting a street lifestyle, the youths were "seeking community, not anarchy" (p. 114). In establishing contact with others like themselves, the youths enacted a process of secondary socialization, adjusting their beliefs and actions to the mores of the street culture.

Relationships with Agency Staff

Youths evidenced a variety of relationships with agency staff, ranging from superficial to exploitative to that approaching surrogate family. Youths' initial contacts with staff tended to be tentative and brief. As youths grew to trust staff members, contacts were longer and more substantive. On occasion, a youth might be persuaded to seek shelter or health care, amenities that had been refused previously. I have represented these relationships in the theme, "I need you and I want to be close but I am so frightened."

Agency staff were often the only nonexploitative contacts street youths had. Vance and other street kids adored one staff member, Kerry. Vance remarked, "A person needs some incentive [to get off the streets]. But if Kerry would even deign to give me a peck on the cheek, I doubt I'd ever recover" (Vance, Log, p. 96.40-43). Another youth proclaimed he came to the piers only to see Kerry, a sentiment which elicited a stern reprimand from Kerry. Bo seemed to seek out agency staff primarily for the purpose of manipulation and exploitation, trying to con coats, shoes, and food. Upon one such unsuccessful attempt, he threw hot chocolate in the face of an outreach worker.

A few youths articulated the importance of their emotional connections with staff:

> [To staff member] You understand what I'm going through. You are the only person who understands (Darryl, p. 22.11-13). [Of another staff member] Medical, mentally, physically, uh, she's always there when I needed her. (Darryl, p. 20.10-12)

> I'm just a boy on the streets and lost, and I have a hard time trusting people, but I am trying to trust Renee and Pam so they can take care of me and find me a place to stay. (Darryl, Log, p. 12.51-54 and p. 13.1-2)

> Maria and Judy, what a pair. We put them through some changes, but they work and work with us, and we all are doing so well. We don't dare come in messed up or they'll read you, child. (Karl, Log, p. 44.53-54 and p. 45.1-3)

Two youths spoke of the resources and sense of refuge proffered by the agency to assist motivated youths in recovery:

> It's location is ideal, right in the midst of everything. I don't have to go to Georgia or upstate New York. I could walk, and really, the entrance is on the ground level, so I mean, it's a gold mine for those who want it (Rick, p. 48.14-21 and p. 49.1-2). This place [the agency, the van] means, uh, security, tranquility, sanity. What do they call it, "Allstate," the helping hand. (Rick, p. 49.6-9)

A place like the Center means a temporary getaway from the streets depending on the person's will or wants to get off of it. See, it's mainly an abusing station so that we can go abuse it for a while to get clothing, food, showers, and then go right back out to where we came from. (Junior, p. 24.6-10)

The van offered a unique sanctuary to the transvestite youths of Cannery Row. I remarked in my field notes that the TV kids "remembered me from week to week and greeted me warmly, welcoming me into their fellowship" (Katherine, Log, p. 34.41-42). I noted in turn that I found these youths "warm, energetic, and stimulating company" (Log, p. 37.25-26), a sentiment that was echoed periodically by other staff. Lindsay, a staff member, expressed the belief that:

The van offered a refuge for the TV kids—a place free of exploitation, violence and ridicule, a place that offered food, fellowship, warmth, and acceptance, and a place for them to get together. (Lindsay, Log, p. 44.41-45)

Upon further questioning, Lindsay articulated her feeling that the Center offered nothing else to the TV kids. They were not allowed to stay at the shelter unless they dressed gender appropriately, they were objects of derision to the straight kids, and they were subject to physical abuse in the predominantly straight male shelter. "The only time," she remarked, "the Center is available for them is when they get AIDS" (Lindsay, Log, p. 45.2-4). Other agencies, particularly those with gay orientations, supported Lindsay's contention that the Center "is notorious for giving gay kids a hard time" (Solotaroff, 1990, p. 34). Indeed, I saw very few transvestite youths during my tenure at the Center. However, other gay and lesbian youths were quick to avail themselves of the services offered by the Center. In spite of this identified shortcoming, the Center and other smaller agencies throughout the City were highly regarded by the media, the public, and the youths themselves, as providing the only effective services available to street kids (Bollinger, 1988a; Hersch, 1988; Solotaroff, 1990). And, it should be noted, the Center was the first, and for several years the only, agency to extend formal housing and hospice care to street youths with symptomatic HIV infection.

Relationships with Mainstream Society

An answer to the subquestion, "What are the relationships of these youths to mainstream society?" emerged in poignant fashion. Three youths expressed the feeling that they were "not normal" with respect to the dominant culture, expressed in the theme "I am not like other people." These feelings reinforced the youths' sense of isolation. This isolation, although occasionally broken on "dates," was not only geographic, but temporal and conceptual:

> People before used to sleep on trains, but you know, kids don't like that. They'd rather find someplace secluded where nobody sees them (Rocco, p. 14.11-14). You, you don't even want to see the daylight, 'cause there's normal people out there and you just don't want it 'cause you feel like you're not normal, especially if you're a prostitute. If you have resolved yourself to prostituting, you feel like you're not normal anymore (Rocco, p. 17.5-12). You isolated yourself from the world itself, from the world itself (Rocco, p. 19.2-6). Yeah, the kids don't feel like they want to be seen by anyone on the outside (Rocco, p. 19.12-13). You're not living a normal life, unless you're working all night and you have the graveyard shift, but you're out there prostituting and hanging out and getting high. (Rocco, p. 20.4-8)

I don't know any regular people. I get to a point where I'm not looking good or my clothes have been stolen, so I can't go out anymore. Plus you're sleeping during the day, so how do you have any time to see regular people, and if I go see anyone, it's like, what do you tell them? What are you doing with yourself? You lose track of a normal lifestyle. You don't know anyone with a normal lifestyle once you begin tricking and you accept it. You accept it, you accept the street as it is. It's how real life is (Junior, p. 18.14-22 and p. 19.1-11). I like going to places to where other people are going. It gets boring though, when it's not your world. Like if I stay with a john for a couple of days or something and we do things or go someplace, it's their world, it's what they're doing. You know, you're living by their rules. (Junior, p. 22.1-11)

I couldn't handle all the classes like going from one class to another class, like all normal people. It just wasn't in my brain. (Louie, p. 10.28-29 and p. 11.1-2)

Several of Sereny's (1985) informants reported that "I never take buses or subways, they're not for me" (p. 74). Sereny explained that her informants, young female prostitutes, "feel out of place in close contact with 'ordinary' people" (p. 74).

This sense of being different, of not being normal, was observed to perpetuate the youths' isolation, in that feeling different, the youths chose to avoid relationships with so called *normal people*. In a similar manner, the nocturnal rhythms of street life limited the youths' exposure to *daytimers* and other ways of being.

The present research largely supported the premise articulated in other studies (Caton, 1986; Deisher & Farrow,

1986; Kennedy et al., 1990; Manov & Lowther, 1983; Office of the Inspector General, 1985; Robertson, J. M., 1988; Wilkinson, 1987) that street youths congregate in isolated areas and seek to avoid contact with mainstream institutions and individuals. The exception to this observation involved youths who prostituted in upscale residential neighborhoods, which phenomenon is addressed in Relationships with Local Residents. Prostitution generally afforded youths nominal contacts with mainstream individuals, described in Relationships with Tricks.

Relationships with the Law

Because my informants often lived outside the constraints of law, they spent considerable time eluding the authorities, and frequently reported being hassled, arrested, or incarcerated.[6] Therefore, police officers and other agents of the judicial system comprised a significant part of their network of acquaintances. I call this theme, "It's a cat and mouse game, me and the cops." The youths' attitudes of tolerance, hostility, and engagement toward *the Law* or *the Man* are expressed in the following passages:

> Officers Kowalski and Mulcahey are out cruising—no money tonight, child! (Unidentified, Log, p. 69.39-42)

> It was you know, they were doing their job, I was doing mine. Of course my job was controversial, so, their job was to lock me up. But you know, they didn't get me for five, six years. They didn't know who I was for five or six years because I was never involved as deeply as I was the last year. And uh, they knew I was, you know, that I wasn't a bad kid. That I didn't go around robbing people and stealing people and tearing up churches and stuff like that, so they basically let me

off like, seven or eight times, and 'cause I've also reported a lot of robberies in the neighborhood and they come to appreciate that, and they see that you're not a bad kid, that you're a victim of circumstance or whatever. Instead of arresting me they would come up to me, 'Rocco, go take a walk' or whatever. (Rocco, p. 17.26-34 and Rocco, p. 18.1-10)

[My gang], we fucked up every cop that came near us . . . Every cat took out 20 cops without a weapon. (Sarah, p. 25.15-18)

Sarah's claim, if a bit exaggerated, nevertheless represents a fantasy of some import. Her assertion may suggest the wished for elements of power and importance, qualities sadly lacking in her day-to-day existence.

Several youths reported that they encountered discrimination and abuse from officers because of their sexual orientations. Another youth alleged that legal proceedings were often unfairly determined because of partiality on the part of lawyers or judges toward particular youths from whom they exacted sexual favors. Sources indicated that police officers, like other professionals, were occasionally involved with youths in more intimate ways:

The bars will close at 2:00 a.m., then things will pick up. The johns that hang out in Rounds and the police who party at Whitney's, they'll be out looking for dates. (Teddy, Log, p.76.4-8)

A small kid stands by the Lincoln Tunnel, he's selling plastic roses for a buck. The traffic's backed up to 39th Street. The TV[7] whores are calling the cops out for a suck. (Reed, 1989)

A few minutes later, Aires stood at the rear of the courtroom engaged in quiet, intense conversation with a young, blond, crewcut officer. When she returned, a friend asked, 'what was that all about?' 'He wants me and Liz to work a stag party for him next Friday.' (Goldsmith, 1993, p. 78)

Weisberg (1985) cited the informal rules of avoiding the law:

When uniformed police approach, walk casually in the opposite direction. Learn to recognize the regular undercover police (p. 31). Ignore anyone who asks you into a car (p. 34). Ask suspicious looking customers if they are police officers, remain silent until the customer makes a proposition and suggests a price and determine if the customer is comfortable when touched. (p. 35)

Sereny (1985) added, "ask him to unzip his fly. . . If they refuse, they're cops." (p. 73)

When Worlds Collide: Relationships with Local Residents

Relationships youths reported with residents of areas they frequented were strained at best, expressed in the theme "They don't like us, we don't like them." Youths engaging in prostitution and drug use disrupted the calm of several residential neighborhoods, introducing to those areas criminal elements, noise and refuse. These intrusions were received with animosity, as two youths recounted.

Oh, they hated me. They hated us. They'd throw hot water out the window, potatoes, hot water, tomatoes, I mean you never know what the hell was gonna come out that window next. I know one time, some hot water or water came down, right, and I looked up, I said, "I'm gonna get you," and there's this little old lady up and there and she goes "Not me, not me, upstairs, upstairs." They do that when you're making a lot of noise too. And on a slow night, there's gonna be a lot of noise on that block, 'cause everybody's hanging out there 'til four or five in the morning. So that's the kind of relationship we have with the residents. (Rocco, p. 18.11-33)

Yeah, everybody here knows us. The residents, the shopkeepers. They harass us, pour hot water out the windows on us. They don't exactly like having us around. (Kyle, Log, p. 22.31-39)

In some areas, residents moved rather than confront the intruders (Gabriel, 1992). In another area, residents established block associations, citizens' patrols and hired private security forces to protect themselves, impelled by escalating assaults, muggings, and murder (*The New York Times*, 1990; Nolan, 1990). A woman who waited tables at a restaurant where the meat packers, paper pushers [business people] and prostitutes often converged for morning coffee summarized the changes–[Since the drug dealers and prostitutes proliferated] "There's a lot of really bad energy. It's a different crowd, much more violent" ("Streets of sanctuary," 1990, p. B1).

The reactions of mainstream society to street youths assumed a different character when the youths were observed at a distance. The media often featured street youths, presenting their stories in a compassionate manner. Less frequently, Jenny and other youths elicited sympathy in observers. On these occasions, the public was observed to respond kindly and generously to youths or to agencies serving them. These divergent responses were noted by other writers (Aptekar, 1988; Kennedy et al., 1990) to be related to whether particular youths were perceived as engaging or threatening to outsiders and varied with the youths' age and maturity.

Prostitution: Freelancing the Public Relations Field

Gus Van Sant (1991) portrayed the world of male hustlers with a credible and occasionally humorous eye in the film, *My Own Private Idaho*. Prostitution, which Junior referred to as "freelancing the public relations field,"[8] commanded a significant position in the lives of my informants, as in the film, in part because it provided a social network and in part because it enabled the youths to pursue more compelling diversions, i.e., getting high. The theme, "I do what I have to do," then, relates the activities of prostitution and getting high. Prostitution is addressed in relation to particular activities, the kids' relationships with tricks, and the dynamics thereof. The phenomenon of bartering sex for drugs occurs at the nexus of drug use and prostitution, and is considered in relation to the culture of crack use in a subsequent section.

Prostitution

Prostitution, then, is a companion activity to drug use for those youths so engaged, enabling youths to support a costly habit with a minimum of effort. Prostitution assumed different guises in different places. Gay males who were less involved in drug use and street life were likely to circulate among patrons of the upscale bars and restaurants of Park Circle. Straight male hustlers and an occasional *butch* gay male pursued *rough trade* around the Wharf, while transvestite males engaged straight and gay identified men on Cannery Row. Young female prostitutes were observed at various locations throughout the City; however, most of my female informants *pulled dates* in and around the Terminal. Although females were observed in some areas to work with pimps, I did not have occasion to speak with these women at length. Male prostitutes were seldom seen to employ an intermediary. The reader is referred to Sereny's (1985) study for a more comprehensive treatment of adolescent prostitutes and their pimps or to Weisberg (1985) for an exhaustive study of male and female prostitution.

A particular street or area where prostitution is practiced is called a *stroll* or *track* (Goldsmith, 1993). "The slow crawl of cars, girls darting into the street, price negotiations at the drivers' windows" (Goldsmith, 1993, p. 65) are common elements of the *stroll*, whether at the upscale Park Circle or downtown at the Wharf.

The ritual behaviors accompanying prostitution are significant. Female "ho's" and transvestites dressed in provocative feminine attire flounced, strutted, and sashayed in exaggerated fashion as they sought to engage tricks; butch or male identified gay males were more subdued in their presentation. Visano (1991) noted that "the boys package themselves as attractive commodities with inviting body language—a grin, prolonged eye contact, and clothing which emphasizes youthful body appearance" (p. 211). Straight male hustlers exhibited a passive demeanor, standing about, waiting for tricks to approach them. The girls and hustlers worked in relative isolation, but prostitution occasioned a celebration for the transvestite youths, a phenomenon addressed in "Pumps and Pearls."

Tricks or *dates*, as prostitute clients are known, constitute the balance of the prostitution equation. In an elaborate mating ritual, a prospective trick would cruise a district at length, appraising each youth for desirability or cleanliness, often circling many times, approaching and withdrawing until a particular youth found favor. Upon agreeing to a date, the trick and youth then negotiated other terms—type of encounter, payment, and use of prophylactics.

The transactions I observed occurred in parked cars or in isolated areas of public spaces. Goldsmith (1993) offers this description:

> Women dash out into the street to flag down cars. On the side streets, in parked cars, one can see heads bobbing up and down.
>
> A girl jumps out of one parked car and into another one so quickly that she might be in a 'Road Runner' cartoon. . . . As [the van] nears its lot, on East Houston Street, it passes a girl in a trenchcoat, which she opens, with the regularity of a windshield wiper, to reveal her naked body. (p. 65)

Less frequently, my informants reported that a date might take a youth home or rent a hotel room (Sarah, p.22.10-12).[9]

Visano's (1991) gay male informants described three types of undesirable clients: *circle jerks*, comprised of older indecisive men who "derive sexual pleasures from watching young hustlers at a distance" (p.221), *gas queens*, who are "impudent single, unattractive, middle-aged, and lonely" (p. 221), and the *lonely old men* who are much "older, cooperative, married . . . and who allow themselves to become emotionally attached. . ." (p. 221-222). Hustlers were said to prefer younger dates, even though older men might offer better terms. Solotaroff (1990), however, suggested a more critical discriminator: "You come down here with twenty bottles (of crack), it doesn't matter how old and ugly you are, you're the Pied Piper of West Street" (p. 37).

To a degree, location determined type of engagement. Congress in cars required blow jobs (Goldsmith, 1993), while fellatio was a matter of convention among bus drivers and crackhouse denizens (Balshem et al., 1992; LeBlanc, 1992)

Couples rented rooms in cheap hotels for more involved activities (Goldsmith, 1993; Sereny, 1985). Tracy identified the *half-and-half*, encounter, so called because it involved "half a blow job and the rest fuck, because it's easier and quicker" (Tracy, p. 18.14-17).

Working the Terminal, Tracy netted five to ten dollars a trick plus crack or fifty dollars without crack. On the docks, youths earned twenty dollars for a blow job, and fifty to one hundred dollars for anal intercourse. Distinctions and concessions were also made depending on whether the youth was the active or passive partner. Louie, speaking vehemently to this concern, said "I don't get fucked, I fuck! And I don't eat cunt!" (Louie, p. 28.16-17). On Morton Street, youths charged fifty to one hundred dollars for an hour with the trick and would "do anything, even S&M" (random field notes). On Park Circle, youths commanded one hundred dollars for a "regular date," and three to four hundred for anything "kinky" (Rocco, p. 39.20). Johns were willing to pay five to ten dollars more for *skin-on-skin*, or sex without condoms (Goldsmith, 1993; Morse, Simon, Osofsky, Balson, & Gaumer, 1991; Solotaroff, 1990; Weatherby et al., 1992), and found many youths receptive, despite its attendant risks.

Although most youths admitted to exchanging sex for drugs, a practice Tracy called *smoking dates* (Tracy, p. 18.4), Rocco cautioned against drug use with a trick, acknowledging the loss of control that might result:

> The tricks take you out, they try to get you high or get you to pass out, so they can take advantage of you. You pass out you are going to wake up bound and tied and beaten. You can't pay for that. Nobody turns a date agreeing to S&M, no amount of money can buy that. You've just got to be careful and not lose control (Rocco, Log, p. 81.33-42). I've known situations where

kids were tortured, tied up, and burned with cigarettes and stuff. They give you the money and leave you unconscious in a doorway or gutter and you don't know what the hell happened. (Rocco, p. 39.21-32)

Louie concurred, stating that

Once they start talking drugs, I take my money first. Because once you get high, you get stupid. I've had people who get high and get stupid and I don't like getting stupid. Using drugs with tricks is very dangerous. I had this one guy picked up a torch, a lighter, and a screw driver. I picked up his baseball bat. (Louie, p. 32.26-31 and p. 33.1-11)

Goldsmith (1993) affirmed that "on the street, danger is omnipresent" (p. 79). She outlined the informal rules of prostitution, framed in the collective wisdom of the streets:

Never enter a car with more than one man in it. Check under the seat for a weapon. Make sure the keys are out of the ignition when you start. Tell him to put his hands on the dashboard, or one on your back and you hold the other. Make sure the doors are unlocked. Don't work if you're high—it can cause an error in judgment. (p. 79)

These admonitions notwithstanding, several researchers reported that drug and alcohol use are an integral part of sexual transactions (Morse, Simon, Balson, & Osofsky, 1992; Morse et al., 1991; Simon et al., 1992; & Visano, 1991). Indeed, John maintained to Weisberg (1985) that prostitution "requires a great deal of fortification with drugs and alcohol." (p. 26.)

Street rape was frequently reported by my female informants, a phenomenon supported by Kennedy et al. (1990), Ritter (1989), Yates et al. (1988), and Yates, MacKenzie, Pennbridge, and Swofford (1991).

Relationships with Tricks

For many street youths, relationships with tricks constituted their primary contact with the dominant culture, and often, their only source of companionship. Two types of relationships with tricks were identified, those based on exploitation or predation and those based on a degree of mutual respect and affection. The former, as Karl, Rocco, and Louie described, tended to involve straight identified males who sought to engage youths in sado-masochistic practices, but many of the latter relationships assumed a mutually supportive quality, such as Louie and Junior described.

Karl's attitude toward abusive tricks was contemptuous:

> See that guy in the brown van? He picks up the kids and wants them to use the bathroom in his mouth, then he wants to kiss them and suck their nipples and stuff. That white car with the man and woman in it? He comes and picks up kids and takes them back to his house over the river so he can watch them fuck his wife. Then he wants to go out and eat Mexican food. (Karl, Log, p. 53.9-19)

Youths were more tolerant of the mutual and respectful relationships that occasionally ensued:

> There's one trick that's over the river. He's a really nice guy. I don't really do anything with him. He helps me out more or less. If I need money, he gives it to me. I go over there if I want to get away from the City,

whenever I want to go. He's a really nice guy and I respect him more than anything. I'd do anything not to hurt him. (Louie, p. 35.17-26)

Solotaroff's (1990) and Visano's (1991) examinations of street kids supported the premise that two types of john and kid relationships exist. Solotaroff reported that:

> Gay men tended to be vastly more benign [than straight identified tricks] to the kids. Many form attachments to their "steadies," bringing them home for several days or even a stretch of weeks before things crap out over drugs or house rules. They'll take a kid out to dinner or occasionally pick him up a shirt, no small favor for someone who's been wearing the same thing all week. Whether it's empathy or romance or rescue fantasy, something quite the obverse of sadism seems to obtain here. (p. 36)

Aptekar (1988) described relationships street children in Colombia had with benefactors. Though mutual assistance rather than sex was the focus of their relationships, other similar qualities were reported, including support, mentoring, and encouragement of the benefactor toward his charge.

Junior and Rocco commented on the variety of contacts that prostitution provided:

> I met various people. I met very influential people. I've met Senators. I've met people in the advertising agencies and I've met, you know, regular people on the street. (Junior, p. 10.6-8)

> All sorts of doctors and lawyers and teachers and principals and cops and detectives and uh, everything.

People on welfare walking up to you, you know, it's strange. (Rocco, p. 38.16-19)

Solotaroff (1990) concluded that although the youths were grateful for the companionship that steady dates offered,

> The experience of being cared for is terrifying to them. On the one hand, they're hungry for it, no matter how long they've been out here, on the other, they're clinging to their badboy swagger, to that uptown street affect by which they survive. "I do what I've gotta do," goes the dogma of West Street, "but I damn sure ain't nobody's boy toy." (p. 37)[10]

Gay or bisexual males comprised the greatest proportion of male prostitutes, whose relationships with tricks are elaborated above. Louie's attitude, expressed in the following passage, typified the attitudes of straight male hustlers.

> I don't have fun with tricks. I have no fun at all. I hate, I'd rather rip them off than do what I have to do. I don't enjoy it one bit. I'm a man. I like girls (Louie, p. 39.12-15). So if they want to pay a couple of hundred bucks, they're stupid idiots. That's all. I don't like 'em. I don't like 'em at all (Louie, p. 44.26-30). And I hate faggots. . . I *hate* faggots. (Louie, p. 14.11-13)

Queer bashing may represent the attempts of some hustlers to

> secure their client's money without engaging in sex. . . By skillfully appraising their client's weaknesses, these boys lure an unsuspecting client into a quiet alley, park, or abandoned building and proceed to beat and

rob him either after or instead of sex. (Visano, 1991, pp. 214-215)

Visano suggests that the excessive violence observed in such encounters may represent "a focused expression of [these youths'] homophobic sentiments" (p. 215).

Jon, uncertain of his sexual orientation, expressed a more ambivalent attitude:

You see, I've got this girlfriend. I've been with her for two years. But I come out here hustling and I feel like I'm starting to like it. I was with this date just now and you know, I really enjoyed it (Jon, Log, p. 63.43-49). It's just so confusing, me starting to like it with guys and not wanting to hurt her. (Jon, Log, p. 64.18-20)

Female prostitutes constituted another distinct group. Limited observations elicited the following views, Sarah's alternately tolerant and exploitative, Tracy's cautious and vulnerable. Paula, like Karl and Louie, was contemptuous of tricks.

I've been tricking since I was thirteen. I saw you could make money out there. Now, tricking, people might think, now what's that with a trick. It's called prostitution and you got a whole bunch of these old men that, who try to take advantage and say, "Well, ten dollars, you know, why not?" (Sarah, p. 1.18-23). I go to a trick's house but these are the ones I trust and I've known for a long time for maybe like years. And they trust me enough to take me to their house. (Sarah, p. 22.9-12)

I'm cautious about getting into cars or just letting somebody stop me off the street. If they look a certain way, I don't mess with them (Tracy, p. 22.16-19). Even if I'm hungry, if they just don't look right to me, I'd be like, "Leave me alone," and I'd yell (Tracy, p. 22.22-26). I've been raped. Once when I was hungry, I've had one guy pull out a knife and take the money back. (Tracy, p. 26.14-19)

And now I have to go out and work my butt off all night pretending I like it, so I can get a room and a couple of bags of dope. I hate men. Do you know I've been raped four times in the past two years? Four times. Do you blame me for wanting out, for wanting to just go to sleep and not wake up? (Paula, Log, p. 50.22-29)

Someone to Want Me

In addition to the positive reinforcements of financial gain and the camaraderie some youths reported, several youths spoke of the sense of empowerment they realized in receiving money and recognition in exchange for their services. This dynamic is illustrated by the theme, "It makes me feel important when people pay money to be with me." Passages in support of this theme follow:

On the East Side, they'll give you anywhere from $50 to $150. [That's not only a lot of money, it's recognition?] Yeah, well, because it feels like you're being wanted by someone . . . Yeah, and a sense of authority. You know, they want you and so, you, you're the power behind it all. Without me, they can't have anything. So it's like, it's a sense of uh, recognition. (Rocco, p. 22.5-16)

I danced in bars, I danced on stage, I mean like in front of a lot of people, men of course, dirty old bucks. It was demoralizing, it was against my upbringing (Rick, p. 2.4-9). But I loved the attention (Rick, p. 6.11-12). I guess I grew before my time. And somebody told me, "people would pay for that. People would pay to see your body." And I was like, "No, you're kidding. Where could I go, where is this place?" And they took me. And all I had to do was get a hard on and get attention and have people want me. That's all I ever wanted was somebody to want me (Rick, p. 6.17-21 and p. 7.1-8). It made me feel important. It made me feel like people looked forward to seeing me and they did. (Rick, p. 7.12-14)

[What keeps me out here?] Well, let's put it this way. It's the sense of power. That I can manipulate men to give me large amounts of money with very little service on my part. Two thousand dollars. They give me their car. In effect, they give me power of attorney over their money and I can give and withhold as I choose (Teddy, Log, p. 76.11-19). I don't just have a lot of self-esteem, but as long as I'm engaged with a trick, I feel real, affirmed. The date's gone, I feel like shit. And let's face it, I don't just have a lot of choices. (Teddy, Log, p. 76.35-39)

Area journalists noted this phenomenon as well:

"I never got any attention at home," says Richie. "And I came out here and everybody looks at me and wants me. I love people to want me. I want people to look at me and want to be like me." (Bollinger, 1988b, p. 19)

"For a lot of the kids, hustling is really a reenactment of what they grew up with, only now they've got the control. Instead of lying in bed helplessly waiting for the parent to come in, now they've got the power to say yes or no—and get paid money to do the thing, on top of it." (Mastroieni, personal conversation with Solotaroff, 1990, p. 34)

Cates and Markley (1992) observed that "hustling may provide a means of attaining control, hence power, over a subgroup of homosexually oriented males perceived as being in more affluent roles" (p. 704).[11]

While V. Price (1989) and Wilkinson (1987) indicated that prostitutes constituted a small minority of the street kid population, Ritter (1989) indicated that the overwhelming majority of street youths engage in prostitution. Several researchers assert that the proportion of youths who turn to prostitution has changed with the advent of crack (Balshem et al., 1992; Ernst & Martin, 1993; Weatherby et al., 1992).

Junior summarized the symbiotic nature of the trick and street kid relationship—"Without them, we wouldn't be there. Without us, they wouldn't be there" (Junior, p. 22.14-15). He then identified his primary motivation for prostitution—"The drugs, the drugs. The only reason I go out there is to make money to get high" (Junior, p. 28.14-16).[12] This is the subject of the next section.

The High Life

I alluded in the previous paragraph to the primacy of drugs in street life. The nihilism street kids evinced in their overall outlooks and which is described in detail in the next chapter, seemed particularly evident in the youths' single minded quest for chemical highs. The theme, "I just got to have it," is at the core of The High Life.

Most street kids' drug of choice is crack, an inexpensive distillate of cocaine. Crack may be cut or mixed with other substances to dilute it. The product is often called a *rock*, and looks like a crumb of plaster or sheet rock. Purchased in small vials with colored caps, crack is smoked in a tubular glass pipe called a *stem* or *bowl*. Some youths collected the vials, or *caps* to resell to the dealer for a nickel apiece while others were known to save them in cracker jack boxes.

A few youths told me that they injected heroin and cocaine intravenously, a combination called a *speedball* or a *crack and smack jam*. The majority of my informants, however, said that they disdained needles, as did Fagan's and Chin's (1991) respondents. Some youths said that they spurned crack, due to its street associations, but admitted to using freebase, a form of smokable cocaine which preceded the large scale manufacture of crack. The use of bazooka, an unadulterated form of crack, was also noted in my sample. Bazooka was said to provide a smoother high and less intense *crash* than crack.

The centrality of drugs, most often crack, permeated every aspect of street kids' lives—encompassing their purpose, their activities, their language, and their friendships. The variety of expressions youths employed to describe different aspects of drug use gives some indication of its importance: *fierce mission, fiending, chasing the dragon, pipe dream,* and *crack dancing* refer to activities related to obtaining crack, getting high, and consequences of using.

Pipe Dreams/Chasing the Dragon

The use of drugs among my informants was first and foremost articulated as an escape mechanism:

I was hurt in my childhood and that had a lot of bearing on what was going on, what's going on now. (Junior, p. 25.10-12)

The abuse started to happen again. So I started to sniff heroin (Louie, p. 6.10-13). I would sniff the heroin and I'd go home, I could handle what was going on. Heroin's the best drug in the world. It makes you relax. It makes you not care about anything. Not a worry in the world (Louie, p. 6.28 and p. 7.1-5). I had been using heroin as an escape and now I use methadone as an escape, but I can function with it, I need it. The heroin numbed my mind to the pain and to the abuse. (Louie, P. 16.29-32 and p. 17.1-2)

Even though I had lots of attention, dancing and turning tricks, I still, there was still something missing, and I thought that feeling of feeling good was what I was missing. And that filled the void. To get high filled the void. (Rick, p. 9.15-19)

V. Price (1989) and others (Goldsmith, 1993; McCarthy & Hagan, 1992; Weisberg, 1985) noted self-medicating in their informants as well, observing that "youths spent most of their money on drugs or alcohol in an attempt to forget painful feelings or low self-esteem" (p. 84).

Fiending

The relentless pursuit of drugs was called a *mission*, an allusion to the Star Trek series (T. Williams, 1989) or occasionally, a *crack attack*:

While on a mission I just go after one trick after another, make the money, and go out and spend it. (Louie, p. 32.3-4)

Young kids live in there, an awful place [a flophouse by the water], and turn tricks and hardly get out for fresh air. I went up in there once and child, it is such a dive. Sometimes I see them come out here in a tizzy, on some kind of fierce mission. They come out in a tizzy looking for drugs, girl, you'd better not get in their way. They come down here on a fierce mission, they'll be robbing you, child. (Karl, Log, p. 53.40-54)

Crack and IV cocaine, powerful stimulants, were so compelling (Weatherby et al., 1992) that youths were known to stay up to the point of physical collapse, turning tricks and getting high, a phenomenon youths called *fiending*. Several youths spoke of their own addictions or that of acquaintances:

Of course, the more money I made, the more dope I used. I got so bad, I would make some money uptown and run downtown to buy and then run back up and do it again. I wore myself out 'til I looked really bad and I didn't care about myself. (Jon, Log, p. 65.49-54)

That kid, Ronnie, is too young. He's too young to be out here. They're killing him, the johns. And he'll do anything, *anything*, for drugs (Kyle, Log, p. 23.20-24). I've got a heroin habit myself, two hundred dollars a day. But I just sniff. I hate needles. (Kyle, Log, p. 23.27-36)

Bo, drug user in extremis, expressed the greatest anguish:

Katherine, it's too late. There's no hope for me. I'll be 21 soon, then what? (Bo, Log, p. 32.3-5). I've got to get into a detox. I want to quit but I can't. And my feet are swoll up and I'm hungry. This stuff's got hold of me and it's making me an animal. I'm doing crazy things, vicious things, things I've never done before. Mugging people and . . . (Bo, Log, p. 31.45-52)

Other researchers confirmed the *total abandon* or disinhibition seen in youths procuring crack: "Now I do anything I can to get money for crack. Rob, beat up, steal, beg, shout. Anything to get money for crack" (Goldstein, Ouellet, & Fendrich, 1992, p. 357). Balshem et al. (1992) cited an informant:

> You have no control, 'til you're down to your last and you don't have nothing else. It robs you, it steals from you, it kills you. I feel you would steal and kill for it. You got no respect for no one, not even yourself. (p. 154)

The Crackhouse

Engagement with the crackhouse culture was reported by only one respondent in my sample, Tracy. She alluded briefly to the chaos she observed there, "people running back and forth, arguing, maybe fighting. And a lot of smoke and whatever" (Tracy, p. 24.31-33).

The crackhouse, like opium dens and shooting galleries of other drug cultures, offers on-site availability of the drug and safe quarters and paraphernalia for drug ingestion—"low prices, fast service, and good quality," according to T. Williams (1989). The crackhouse is often quartered in an abandoned building or housing project, guarded from intruders by the *lookout* and from dishonest customers by bodyguards (T. Williams). The odor of feces and urine often permeates crackhouses, many of which lack the amenities of plumbing and electricity (Murphy & Rosenbaum, 1992; T. Williams, 1989). Users often stay in the crackhouse for days at a time, until resources are depleted or exhaustion ensues.

Men are reported to visit crackhouses for two purposes—to procure and smoke crack, and to exploit the availability of sex with women crack users (Balshem et al., 1992). Women, having fewer resources than men, are drawn to the crack house to obtain crack through the exchange of sex for drugs, a practice called *trading* (Balshem et al., 1992; Goldstein et al., 1992, Murphy & Rosenbaum, 1992). These women, ranking low in the drug hierarchy, are variously called *strawberries, skeezers* (Goldstein et al., 1992), *crack stars*, or *rock stars* (Balshem et al., 1992). The term *rockhouse tossups* (Balshem et al., 1992; Goldsmith, 1993; Goldstein et al., 1992) illustrates the harsh attitude of male users toward traders, women "who are to be used for sex acts and then tossed away" (Goldsmith, 1993). In some cases, as with Rocco's sister who was thrown off a roof, the term is quite literal.

Women may also engage in bartering in rockhouses to avoid "the hazards of copping drugs in the illicit marketplace" (Goldstein et al., 1992), a concern noted by Tracy:

> I got locked up once, just getting into somebody's car. It turned out to be a cop (Tracy, 22.10-12). I'm scared to pick up just anybody (Tracy, 22.5). So I'm cautious about getting into a car, or just letting somebody stop me off the street . . . If they look a certain way, I don't mess with 'em. (Tracy, 22.16-19)

Trading is usually in the form of fellatio, or *sporting* in the vernacular of the streets (Balshem et al., 1992). In theory, sex is proffered for crack is in units of time measured by a burning cigarette; however, it is not uncommon for men to deny payment on completion of services (Murphy & Rosenbaum, 1992).

Crack Dancing

Tracy also told me about a phenomenon known as *crack dancing*, a means by which crack users stay awake during a long binge:

> Some people when they stay up, you know, overnight or they stay up for two days, they, they're rocking. You know, things like they dance, like they call it the crack dance. And you can't stop moving (Tracy, p. 20.23-27). It's like a way of keeping yourself awake. You gotta see it to believe it. They want to stay up so they can smoke some more (Tracy, p. 21.13-18). And people, they're fighting it for some what reason. They're fighting sleep.   They're fighting something. They just don't wanna go no where else but right there and they wanna smoke. They can't stop for hours. (Tracy, p. 26.5-11)

An outreach staffer, Hector, made this observation upon watching a kid wearing a walkman, alone on the pavement, dancing like he was possessed:

> Look at that, would you? Look what that stuff will make you do. Out here dancing like some kind of dervish. . . What would I ever want to quit this job for? Where else you going to see anything like that? No sir, I'll be the last one leaving when this place closes down. (Hector, Log, p. 34.10-20)

Goldsmith (1993) offers this description and explanation of crack dancing:

> At the corner of Jerome Avenue and 182nd Street, the crack dance commences: a cafe-au-lait girl in a brocaded jacket moves spasmodically, her arms flying

out at random angles, her eyes darting from the van to the street, where cars move slowly past. . . Outside the window, a rail-thin, sallow woman bobs rhythmically up and down, as if on a spring. . . 'See how they twitch?' [an observer] says. 'What you see is a lack of muscle control, an automatic [sic] response. That's what crack does to them. (p. 74)

Several other observations are noted with respect to crack. The phenomenon of *ghost busting* refers to the practice cited by Sarah (personal conversation, 1988) in which crack users scrutinize themselves and their environment for crumbs of overlooked rock. LaBlanc (1992) alluded to the factitious lesions many crack users manifest:

Trina's skinny scabby arm gropes out from under a stained blanket that reeks of rotten meat. . . Then she picks at the scabs on her legs, circling the faded purple marks with a pen. "Crackpocks!" she laughs. . . (LeBlanc, 1992, p. 28).[13]

Trina also acknowledged the mood swings common in heavy crack users, calling "her bad moods her 'crack ache' " (LeBlanc, 1992, p. 30).

Crack users, appetites suppressed and activity excited by the drug's stimulant effect, evidenced unorthodox eating habits, described by LeBlanc (1992):

When she would eat, which was infrequently, she would binge—two Quarter Pounders, a cheeseburger, a shake, two large fries, apple pie, cookies, and a large Coke™. She hoarded sugar and ketchup packets and poured handfuls of half-and-half cups down her throat, two at a time. (p. 26)

Indeed, during the years of my employment at The One, I observed Sarah gain and lose many, many pounds related to her use of or occasional abstinence from crack. Many youths wore multiple layers of heavy clothing summer and winter to conceal their extreme weight loss.

In addition to the cardiac and neurologic effects evidenced by cocaine users, crack users suffered the unique effects of *crack stomach,* for stomach irritation or gastritis, and *crack lung,* which describes the state of respiratory distress and peculiar radiographic findings that result from aerosol ingestion of crack fumes.

Other descriptions of the crack lifestyle may be found in T. Williams' (1989) treatise, *Crackhouse: Notes from the End of the Line,* and R. Price's (1992) fictionalized account of the crack culture, *Clockers.*

Alcohol

Most of my informants partook freely of alcohol, but alcohol use was taken for granted and seldom remarked on.[14] Darryl alone professed use of alcohol only. V. Price (1989) observed that her informants considered alcohol and marijuana use a lifestyle rather than drug abuse, a term those youths reserved for harder substances, most commonly cocaine.

Discussion

Researchers posit a variety of explanations for the apparent rise in drug use. Fagan and Chin (1991) and Goldstein et al. (1992) argue that changing market forces and the intrinsic properties of crack have altered the established patterns and rituals associated with drug initiation and use in the direction of chaos and anarchy. Prior to the introduction of crack, young people were introduced to drugs by acquaintances or friends in a milieu of warmth and friendship (Fagan & Chin). The rules of proper drug use and acceptable behavior were communicated by experienced peers to the novice user. With the advent of the intense but transient crack high, its relative affordability and immediate accessibility, the phenomenon of drug use as a shared ritual among friends gave way to the dealer mediated, asocial overdrive of crack (Fagan & Chin).

The phenomenon of trading initiated by crack users has brought dramatic changes to the practice of prostitution. Presumably, more individuals are participating in the exchange of drugs-for-sex than were previously engaged in traditional prostitution (Balshem et al., 1992; Weatherby et al.,1992), effecting a buyer's market for services and driving down prices (Balshem et al., 1992; Goldstein et al., 1992). Many proponents of traditional prostitution contigm the women who exchange sex for drugs, in part because the traders violate the implicit code of professional prostitutes that "one provides services for money and buys one's drugs as an independent matter" (Balshem et al., 1992, p. 150), and in part because traders comply with the degrading and demeaning demands of customers and accept minimal compensation (Goldstein et al., 1992).

Crack related trading has also had the interesting effects of excluding the pimp from sexual transactions, and boosting the power and influence of the crack dealer or holder (Goldstein et al., 1992). Morningstar and Chitwood (1987) indicated that "the cocaine dealer was replacing the pimp as the man of status on the streets. . . A man can hardly make a woman do anything now. A woman is for herself. . . and just makes love for cocaine with dudes that have coke" (p.138). Other writers (Balshem et al., 1992; Murphy & Rosenbaum, 1992) politicized the asymmetrical balance of power that obtains in trading, arguing that inequitable distribution of resources and opportunity sustains the drugs-for-sex connection.

Several researchers commented on the emergence of the crack endemic in the '80s in the context of social and economic upheaval. Pervasive poverty, deteriorating social organization, and diminished life opportunities in the inner city created a milieu in which drug dealing has evolved as a reasoned and legitimate career (Balshem et al., 1992; Fagan & Chin, 1991; Goldstein et al. , 1992), and drug use is perceived as a means of transcending relentless need (Balshem et al., 1992; Murphy & Rosenbaum, 1992).

Drug use, which Wilkinson (1987) called *partying*, or "getting high, getting stoned" was seen in her typology as a social activity. She stated that "it was difficult to understand the attraction that drinking and getting high held for [the street kids]" (p. 111). In the end, she compared the practice to that of "the bar scene" in the dominant culture. Aptekar (1988) indicated that drug use was not a central feature of street life in Colombia, but that a few children became involved with drugs to mask their depression. One child told him, "[the polish] made me feel dizzy, but I liked to smell it because it helped me forget how hard it is to live on the streets" (p. 72).

No one of these views seems sufficient to explain my observations of the street youths of my acquaintance. The pervasive use of crack and the extremes to which youths would go to obtain crack suggest that crack has introduced a new element to the conundrum that street kids present—that of endemic hard core addiction. Sante (1992) submits the premise that "drugs impose their own structure—customs and language, goals and priorities, rewards and punishments—on lives in which all belief has collapsed, and with it conventional structures" (p. 23). This observation, which couples social and emotional components with the physiology of addiction,[15] provides an intriguing explanation to the question of why street kids stay on the streets. As Deborah observed, "The crack keeps calling me back" (Deborah, audiotape).

Survival Strategies

The disruption of the developmental sequence thrust on street kids requires that they assume adult responsibilities for sustenance, safety, and shelter. Some writers spoke of the resourcefulness street kids bring to the task (Luna, 1991; Manov & Lowther, 1983; McCarthy & Hagan, 1992; V. Price, 1989), an interpretation which Kennedy et al. (1990) suggested "implies mature judgment," arguing instead that street kids must survive in an adult world with the resources of a child, often "making wrong and tragic choices" (p. 86). The categories which follow, Getting By, and Sleeping Arrangements, and Breaking Night specifically address the research Subquestions, "What survival strategies do street youths use in coping on the streets?" and "What tacit knowledge enables them to survive?"

Getting By

The efforts youths brought to their struggle for subsistence are expressed in the themes "I can take care of myself," or "I have ways to get along." Few of the present informants admitted to panhandling, but prostitution, dealing and scamming were readily acknowledged. Legitimate employment and theft were also described.

One girl, Jenny, who manifested overt psychiatric illness, lived in a 24-Hour Automatic-Teller space, where customers, perhaps reminded of their own fortune, passed her five and ten dollar bills. She was so spared from the more onerous burden of procuring an income by other means.

Street youths of my study commonly if not universally resorted to prostitution, discussed more completely in previous sections, as the preferred mode of gaining income. This endeavor required no education or overhead and if it was somewhat risky, the high earnings seemed to compensate.

Proponents of this activity remarked on the easy money prostitution brings:

> I'm going to make some money now, child. I'm going to take off these pants (hot pants) and put on this skirt (pulling a shirred brown miniskirt from her bag) and make me some money. Now are you coming or not? (Rhonda, Log, p. 5.38-45)

> Upon being asked whether they (a group of transvestite girls) do this for the money or for drugs, informants responded in one voice, "Money!" "Money, child!" (Unidentified, Log, p. 69.46-49)

> I can go out and make what people make in a week, I can make in an hour, and blow it in the same day (Louie, p. 38.16-18). It's found money (Louie, p. 38.27), no respect money. It took you 15 minutes to make two hundred dollars, what kind of respect you going to have for it? Its not like I had to work in an office for 40 hours to get that two-hundred dollars. (Louie, p. 39.2-5)

Louie described procuring young males for sexual congress with older men: "I do it 'cause I need the money and they're out there anyway trying to sell themselves so why don't I just do them a favor?" (Louie, p. 24.33-35).

Several researchers (Deisher, Farrow, Robinson, & Boyar, 1982; Inciardi, 1984; Schaffer & DeBlassie, 1984) identified economic factors manifested in "easy money" as the prime motivator for prostitution, a conclusion supported by my research. Further, most of my respondents acknowledged that their engagement in prostitution was motivated by drug procurement rather than survival.[16]

A hustle or scam implies a scheme by which one gains money or goods in a fraudulent manner or "maximizing gain with a minimum of effort" (Visano, 1991, p. 209). Youths sometimes referred to this activity as "running a game" or "taking the edge" (ibid). Informants universally described or evidenced various hustles or scams. Subway tokens were highly valued as they could be bartered or exchanged for currency. Youths often sought to con outreach workers for tokens, as Seth's plea illustrates: "I've got a bad leg, I can't walk on it, man. I've got to get back home to my mom. Can't you give me a token?" (Seth, Log, p. 33.46-52). Goods were sometimes secured for personal use; more often for resale. Bo, recipient of dozens of shoes and coats, claimed that "My coat, the other coat you gave me, got stolen. Please give me another one, it's cold out here!" (Bo, Log, p. 27.13-16). Attempts to manipulate staff were manifold, as with Bo's pledge to enter detox in exchange for food. Outreach staff were equally adept at recognizing a hustle, as Kerry demonstrated with her response to Seth's request for tokens: "Just who do you think you're talking to?! Do I look like your fool? Now don't give me no more of that bullshit!" (Kerry, Log, p. 33.54, 34.1-3).

The youths were most creative in hustling food. Darryl would enter a restaurant or store, "and lie and say I'm diabetic or something because I need sugar in my system" (Darryl, p. 11.20-22), a story good for ongoing assistance. Sarah, who exudes an animal sensuality, upon entering a bodega or store, would sweet talk the clerk:

> 'Yo, how you doing, Keith, you know you're big and strong, I'll come back, and I'll treat you right.' It's a lie. I sucker these guys out of food (Sarah, p. 21.2-6). I'll never come back and treat 'em right. And I'll be walking out with twenty dollars worth of food and never come back. (Sarah, p. 21.14-15)

Rocco,[17] a dapper and handsome young Latino, reported that:

> Stealing is easy in the winter time cause we have these big coats, you know. And you stick the merchandise down your pants and close your coat up and you know, you flirt with the employees, you know, not sexually. I mean, you know, "do you have this, do you have that?" and the next thing you know they go, "Well, no, try across the street," and they like, send you out of the store with their merchandise. (Rocco, p. 33.25-32 and 34.1-2)

McCarthy and Hagan (1992) reported that their informants spoke of other means of food procurement. A *bun run* refers to taking food from a delivery truck as it is parked for unloading (p. 422), while *dine and dash* describes dining at a restaurant, then departing without paying (p. 422).

Darryl, an enterprising youth, stated:

> I have a lot of credit out there. I can get something from the store and pay it back. You know they don't bug me about it but I always pay it back (Darryl, p. 9.13-16). And sometimes I beg or sometimes I hand out flyers and sometimes I go to people when they are entering their apartments and ask them if they would donate any clothes. (Darryl, p. 10.19-22)

Sarah and other informants also reported *vicing* or victimizing their tricks—"I don't turn tricks—I vic them!" (Sarah, p. 11.9-10). In Sarah's case, this could take the form of *snagging* a wallet or a more menacing form, as when Sarah would enter a vehicle, ostensibly to turn a trick, then her partner, a "big goon or barbarian" (Sarah, p. 12.16-17) would come out to the car 'Boom boom boom. What are you doing in there with my cousin? Get out of there!' You know, you scared the daylights out of him. And he's like, 'Give me all your money! Boom boom boom. Leave her alone, she's underage.' It's like, fun. (Sarah, p. 12.2-8)

And in this fashion, rough up the john and relieve him of his money and valuables. Bond et al. (1992) and Goldstein et al. (1992) affirmed this practice—"many times if they smoke a log, the urge is taken away and I don't even have to give the sex" (p. 356).

Purse-snatching and more sophisticated theft and burglary were also described. One rather hardened youth, a hustler in rough trade, recounted many muggings:

I don't go for the weak people. Old people and cripples. That's low. I go for somebody who can fight back, somebody strong. I tell them "give me your money." If they refuse, I tell them, "give me your money or I'll hurt you." They don't come through, they want to resist, I hit them in the knees with a stick. I hurt them bad. And I take their money and their watches and jewelry. They learn. I get their credit cards, oh, child, I love that plastic. I can work a credit card, it will bring tears to your eyes. I work that thing 'til it bleeds. (Gray, Log, p. 97.1-12)

During my earlier work with street kids, I discerned another means youths had of acquiring goods, a theme I have called "When I need something I go shopping." On occasion a youth would remark that he needed clothes or toiletries and inform me in a most dramatic fashion, "I'm going shopping at Barney's." Jay showed me a parcel and said, "I've been shopping at Lord and Taylor's." *Shopping* in this context communicated a sardonic reference to shoplifting. *Boosting* was another term the kids used for shoplifting or stealing. The casual and accepted nature of shoplifting was underscored when a youth specified he had actually bought particular merchandise, waving a receipt at me to substantiate his claim. The *U.S. News and World Report* ("Armani or your life," 1992b)[18] noted that gangs of transvestite youths have expanded operations to the theft of couture clothing for Ball competitions.[19]

Dealing drugs was an occasional, if hazardous, vocation. Deborah said: "Yeah, I be dealing some. But not this nickel and dime stuff. I run it, carry a big bundle from one place to another. Not on the streets where you get caught and get robbed and go to jail" (Deborah, audiotape). Sarah, a retailer, was known to rip off her distributor to support her own heavy crack use—"I broke out with 39 bundles since 1988. That is $3,900 in drugs" (Sarah, p. 14.11-12), admitting however that the distributor then dispatched agents who beat her up and drove over her. Louie started running heroin at 12 years of age:

> I could run a package that was 5 bundles of 10, which is 100 bags. I would run it to the dealer and get a couple of bags for doing it. And I would run all day. Back and forth, packages, packages, packages, all over the city. I was making good money. (Louie, p. 7.7-13)

On occasion, a youth reported legitimate, if marginal, employment. Darryl had worked cleaning movie theaters in return for admission and had worked at intervals as a messenger and handing out flyers. Many gay youths had worked for escort services or as dancers at X-rated shows. A few youths had worked at various fast food emporiums. Most such employment was episodic and opportunities for gainful employment diminished as the youths' appearance deteriorated with drug use, weight loss, and street life.

Two notable exceptions to the above are noted: Rocco, more functional than most street youths of my acquaintance, worked as a bookkeeper at respectable businesses between his extended forays. Heriberto, an accomplished *voguer* and member of the House of Balanciaga,[20] had just appeared on the Black Entertainment Network, where he performed this disciplined art form. Soon after I made Heriberto's acquaintance, he and a select group of other young dancers accompanied a rock superstar on a music video and concert tour.

By way of contrast, I often saw older street people collecting and redeeming aluminum cans or begging on trains. A number of adult males were also observed packaging rocks or newspapers inside electronic equipment boxes, then hawking them to unwary consumers as videocameras and such. Aptekar (1988) reported that in addition to such scams as dirtying windshields so as to be paid for cleaning them, Colombian street children evolved reasoned businesses, cleaning and recycling ice cream sticks, or renting ladders to the bereaved, enabling mourners to place wreathes on elevated grave sites. Whereas Colombian street children worked in small groups called *camadas*, the present informants generally worked haphazardly, in isolation or with one partner.

Martin (1982), who studied patterns of adaptation among urban transient females, identified five basic survival needs: food, clothing, shelter, money, and personal hygiene. Martin's respondents relied largely on charitable organizations in securing survival needs, a network Kufeldt and Nimmo (1987) called "the street welfare system," and to a lesser extent on panhandling. Wilkinson (1987) identified panhandling, prostitution, drug dealing, and scamming as the predominant means by which street kids acquire needed materials.[21] T. Williams (1989), who studied the residents of a crackhouse, related their patterns of procurement to those of earlier societies of hunters and gatherers, a metaphor equally descriptive of my informants. The present study elaborates on and largely concurs with Martin's and Wilkinson's work with respect to "getting by."

Several sources indicate that poor school performance, high dropout rates, and absence of marketable skills limit legitimate employment opportunities for street kids (Balshem et al., 1992; Goldsmith, 1993; Murphy & Rosenbaum, 1992; Wurzbacher et al., 1991; Yates et al., 1991). As Teddy commented, "Let's face it, I don't just have a lot of choices" (Log, p. 76. 38-39).

Sleeping Arrangements

Securing a safe place to sleep was of some concern to my informants, but with judgment compromised by drug use, the youths sometimes slept wherever they dropped:

> I crash in the park or on the train. In a regular house, a trick's house. . . But these are the ones that I trust and I've known for a long time for maybe like years. (Sarah, p. 22.6-10)

> You would sleep wherever you could find security. I mean an abandoned house or under a bridge by the water. Somewhere where you could be secure, where nobody sees you. (Rocco, p. 14.8-14)

> I was doing it [dancing] to keep my hotel room together. It was thirty bucks a night and I could make that easy. It was a sleazy hotel, but better than the streets. (Rick, p. 8.12-15)

> I try to go to sleep during the day, that way I won't have no hoodlums roaming around me at night. I don't

sleep during the night while they're roaming the street. (Tracy, p. 15.19-24)

Solotaroff (1990) noted that until street kids are sheltered, "they will go on wintering on the E Train, or at a certain all-male theater in the Village" (p. 37). One youth told him:

> You go in expecting to see a whole bunch of bizarre sex going on, and instead it's all these young kids knocked out sleeping. In the middle of February, you'll be glad they let you stay there, but those seats get hard on your ass, boy (p. 37).

These locations are similar to what V. Price (1989) and Wilkinson (1987) described with respect to sleeping arrangements.

Two youths of my acquaintance had made a home in the back of an abandoned garbage truck, "furnishing the truck with a mattress, blanket and chair, and putting carpet down where trash used to line the floor" (Bollinger, 1988, p. 23).[22] As many as a hundred youths had at one time established quarters in a warehouse, the "Salt Mines," where the City stored salt, "sleeping and playing in close proximity to the rats they called 'the Fat Boys' " (Bollinger, 1988a, p. 23). One youth remarked to Solotaroff (1990):

> They had the most casual rats in there. Big-ass ones that walked right up to you and started chewing on your shit. If you count my father, I've slept with sick dirty bastards for 13 years, but rats I cannot work with. (p. 37)

These youths were displaced, but not housed, when public outrage provoked by the Bollinger (1988a, 1988b, 1988c, 1988d) series on street youths exposed the City to public censure. Ironically, many youths who could not obtain housing by reason of their homelessness, have now been sheltered by reason of AIDS.

Aptekar (1988) observed that Colombia's street children knew that nights would be long and that when and where they might sleep was problematic. Their fear of night compelled them to "sleep as we were able, pressing together to stay warm, while encouraging each other to guard against the panic we all have" (p. 117). The younger children of his study manifested nightmares, bed-wetting, and thumb-sucking, evidence of the disruption of the developmental sequence and their vulnerability. The children reported that their episodic use of alcohol or inhalants helped them to sleep at night.

Breaking Night

Related to sleeping was the phenomenon of breaking night. An informal ritual, breaking night referred to the practice of "hanging out all night long without going to sleep" (Sarah, p. 19.12-13), usually because the youths were "making money and getting high" (Tracy, p. 21.18-20). On occasion, however, the youths had no place to stay and preferred to walk all night rather than risk the vexation of a vagrancy citation. Walking exacted its own penalties for youths walking in the cold with poor fitting shoes and well worn socks, an observation confirmed by Moy and Sanchez (1992). I came to call the resulting condition of macerated feet, tinea, and secondary infection the "Bo Syndrome" after first observing the complex in the beleaguered Bo.

For Rocco, breaking night had negative connotations, because it meant "you're not living a normal life" (Rocco, p. 20.4-5), though his friends thought it a good thing, bragging about how much crack they had done. Wilkinson (1987) noted that her informants also were relieved to maintain a high for several days at a time because it obviated the need to find a place to sleep. Breaking night had a parallel in Aptekar's (1988) notion of *illeca*. This term, according to his informants, "wanted to mean passing the night on the streets, but it is more like day with fear on top of it" (p. 117).

Group Life and Solitary Life

Group life among street kids took several forms. A hierarchy is described in response to observed and reported patterns of interactions among various street youths. Two particular forms of group life are elaborated, one being the pattern of life which evolved among a small group of street kids who occupied a lean-to over the river, and the other being the group dynamics of transvestite youths observed on the van and around Cannery Row. A third life experience, that of Tracy, is interposed by way of contrast to represent the solitary existence many street youths chose.

The Hierarchy

Several observations led me to posit the existence of a hierarchy among street kids. On one occasion, I had invited three of my informants to lunch for the purpose of "member checking" my analysis. Two youths, Junior and Rocco, were Hispanic, attractive, well groomed, articulate, and projected confidence and poise. In contrast, Angela was quiet and shy, a pretty but worn appearing blond transvestite, with an extraordinarily feminine appearance. Angela seemed by far the more damaged child with respect to abilities, resources, and background. Upon hearing that Angela was joining us for lunch, Rocco and Junior verbalized their dismay, and neither spoke to nor acknowledged Angela throughout our engagement.

Second, I had heard and my observations confirmed that separate and distinct groups of youths frequented certain areas.

Park Circle and its gay bars attracted youths who could travel in a more upscale social milieu. These youths were more restrained in their drug use, relatively more intact emotionally, and demonstrated considerably more concern with their hygiene and appearance than the youths who inhabited the Terminal or hung out on the piers. Solotaroff (1990) captured this phenomenon in a vivid manner:

> If you are sitting on that wall at two in the morning, the cold and damp on you like a molestation, chances are you aren't one of the sleek-skinned kids who turns up here on weekends for the party off of Christopher Street. Chances are even better that you aren't one of the buttoned-down 20 year olds hustling a place like Rounds on 53rd Street, presenting your business card—Professional Escort—to the Aquascutum crowd. No, the chances are you are what they call a "dead boy" down here—a throwaway between the ages of 16 and 20, homeless and hungry, and like as not, in ill health. (p. 34) [23]

Other discriminants which supported the existence of a street hierarchy were the willingness of some youths to sleep anywhere, the willingness of many youths to make a direct exchange of sex for as little as a five dollar vial of crack, and the extreme practices some youths would endure to obtain drugs. Rocco commented:

> I'm not gonna say I've done it all, but I've been asked to do it all. Some of it's just too disgusting. At the beginning it was your normal basic sex (Rocco, p. 38.30-352). . . but then again, you still have your demented ones out there that tell you to do this stuff that's just grossly out of this world, out of tune with your brain, you know. Which I of course refused to do (Rocco, p. 39.4-8). I've known of a few situations

where kids have been tortured and tied up and burned
with cigarettes and I told them like 'Why do it?' (Rocco,
p. 39.21-25). I've been offered to work for an escort
agency, but I said to hell with that, that's like pimping.
I'd never tolerate that, shit no. (Rocco, p. 40.12-14)

Whereas youths on the upper rungs of the hierarchy
disdained such desperation, youths in the lower echelons of the
street were likely to deny such distinctions even while
admitting to extremes of behavior. Deborah hurried to deny
such an order with respect to sleep, stating, "There's no
differences between us, I just find a blanket and lie down
anywhere" (Deborah, audiotape). Brian, whom I engaged as a
member checker, referred to the "act as if, come as if"
phenomena, that is, one assumed the values and attitudes
appropriate to the location and could change these at will.
Morse et al. (1991) concurred with Brian, stating that "the only
meaningful difference between a bar hustler and street
prostitute was where he happened to be standing at the
moment" (p. 536). Some youths were seen over a period of
time and with accelerated drug use to devolve from a higher
level to a lower one within the hierarchy.

Solotaroff (1990)[24] implied another observation, that the
types of johns varied somewhat by location as well, dynamics
which contributed further to the position of youths in the
hierarchy. If Park Circle attracted the upscale businessman who
could pay dearly for sex with young boys, the piers were
populated by johns of leaner economic means and straight
identified and married men from across the river. Youths who
could command the attention and resources of wealthier tricks
on the Circle looked down on the Terminal kids who engaged
in "unseemly five dollar sexual encounters" (Weisberg, 1985,
p. 37), or who would "give it away" for a vial of crack. Even a
youth's drug of choice might reflect on his or her position in the

hierarchy, as more discriminating users smoked only freebase and the more desperate youths smoked the cheaper crack.

Visano (1991) indicated that younger gay hustlers were in greater demand than more seasoned youths, due to their "youthful energy, spontaneity, and naive sensuality" (p. 213). He elaborated:

> Years on the street, drug use, long hours on street corners, poor nutritional habits, inadequate sleep, heavy cigarette smoking, anxieties concerning subsistence, and the affliction of sexually transmitted diseases exact a price on the physical well-being and attractiveness of a hustler. Further, young hustlers are more likely to engage the affections of younger tricks, while older hustlers must make concessions to negotiate liaisons with older, less desirable clients. (pp. 213-214)

Goldsmith (1993) described a hierarchy among female prostitutes, some of whom

> sell sex for money, others for drugs; and still others use sex to survive (p. 66). At the top of the hierarchy are 'call girls' and 'escort service girls' who tend to have a somewhat predictably private clientele (p. 66). At the bottom of the heap are the homeless, often substance abusers, who find street walking a way to survive. (p. 67)

Aptekar (1988) identified a hierarchy within the *galledas* or groups in which his informants worked. The *jefe* was the boss who maintained power over the other youths by providing food, clothes, and entertainment to his charges, and when necessary, by physical force. The *jefe* was, however, indebted to the younger children for their contributions, as they were more effective at evoking sympathy and eliciting donations than the older youths.

The Club House

Two of my informants described for me their shared existence in a lean-to known as the Club House. I have created in the following paragraphs one story from elements of theirs.

I'm the founder of the Club House which I started three years ago. Now it's so hot you need a Gold Card to get in. It's sort of like you're living outside, but it's under a roof and we have real beds, we call them huts that we live in. There's one older guy, a Rastafarian, who's lived there for seven or eight years. Before we got there, he didn't know anything about cooking meals or staying warm. Now, about nine other people live there, via the Census Bureau.

Anyway, three years ago I was on a little mission. I didn't have anywhere to go to smoke my crack and as I was walking by the Bridge I noticed a gate across the street, next to the heliport. Out of curiosity I crossed over and found this big wooden shipping crate, with a mattress right inside it. Needless to say, I stayed there to do my drugs. The next night I was wondering "Damn, where am I going to sleep tonight?" and boom, I remembered that mattress and thought, "Why not go back?" That's how me and three other friends started the place, three years ago. In the winter, we'd go away, but in the summer, it was the Club House.

Even if we had other places to stay, we'd go there on weekends, but the more we got on drugs, the more it got to be like permanent housing. Then we started showing one kid and he'd show another kid and the next thing you know, we had a tenants' association. I mean, eight or ten people were living there with double beds and bunk beds. Now there's benches, beds, dressers, mirrors, we even set up a fireplace, using an old metal utensil drawer. For water, we got these twenty gallon containers and carried them across the street to the pump and that would pretty much last us all night. We could cook everything, rice and beans, macaroni, chicken stew, pork chops, steaks. Things we stole at the store. We use candles for light when it's dark. For money we hustled, for clothes we turned to The One. Now when I see kids that need a place to stay, I send them to the Club House. What we have in common, besides living on the streets, is drugs. We live a day-to-day life of drugs. Bazooka now, we're all reformed crack heads. It's a better high, you come down easier than with crack.

A typical day, after being out all night, we'd come home at seven in the morning and go to sleep. When we woke up, we might go get doughnuts at the diner on Second Avenue, the guy there gives us all his doughnuts at the end of the day. So we'd go get the doughnuts and from there we'd go over mopping, hopping and mopping,[25] as we say. Go in a store and steal a couple of steaks and get everything we need and go back to the Club House and cook and eat. Then maybe we'd take a nap or wash our clothes in the fire hydrant and get everything ready for that night. Then we'd go to sleep and wait 'til dark. In the summertime we've got to wait 'til the sun goes down to go out on Park Circle or else we go to the Alley. Out there the money is less and you smoke your crack with your date, but it's easier than getting ten dollars and coping, then turn another date and another date. On Park Circle, it's more fun and you might make fifty dollars an hour, you might make a hundred and fifty. But in the summertime, everybody leaves town and there's less people around.

Discussion

The authenticity of this form of group life was supported by a member checker, Brian, who had lived with his friends in another abandoned building. V. Price (1989), alluded to this practice, but noted that violence and carelessness posed many hazards for occupants.

Wilkinson (1987) alluded to group life only with respect to those few youths who were able to let an apartment, which they shared with other street kids with the expectation of shared responsibilities. She also remarked on "partying," that is drinking and getting high, as a shared activity.

Nerlove and Roberts (cited in Aptekar, 1988) developed the concept of "natural indicators of intelligence," defined by "competence in the local subculture" (p. 31). These indicators included

> knowledge of the natural environment, including the ability to move around at considerable distances away from their homes and neighborhoods, the ability to engage in productive self-managed and nonsupervised activities, the ability to initiate and complete tasks, and the social awareness of people. (p. 31)

Aptekar credited his informants with a high degree of native intelligence. Although there is controversy in the literature about the resourcefulness of street kids, I believe that in creating a living space, in procuring and preparing food, in acquiring clothing, and in exploiting available resources such as the Center, Junior and Rocco demonstrated a considerable, if primitive, degree of creativity and self-sufficiency.[26] These qualities further attest to the tacit knowledge street youths possess with respect to survival. Rocco and Junior were more functional in these respects than Tracy, whose story follows, and other more damaged youths.

Solitary Life

In contrast to the sociable and gregarious demeanor Rocco and Junior projected, many other youths evinced a solitary existence, devoid of contact with peers. I asked Tracy to describe a typical day for me. Her story went like this.

First thing, when I've been up all night, I scrape up a dollar or change and get something to put on my stomach, but usually I'd have to do something for somebody to get that. I'd go to the Deli on the Avenue and get a cup of coffee and a buttered roll or a cake. In the mornings I take about five cups of coffee, sometimes because I'm cold, sometimes I just have a taste for it. If I had any money left over, I'd buy a vial of crack. Then I go try to hide in the Terminal, where no one can find me. I try to sleep during the day when there's no hoodlums running around. There's other kids sleeping on the floor, but we don't have nothing to say to each other unless it's "Move over," or "Can I borrow your blanket." When I wake up around three or four o'clock, I try to go to the Center to get something to eat or maybe a shower and clean clothes, but most times I don't even make it through security, because I come there so much and keep going back out. If I wake up later, 'cause I was up really late, I probably wouldn't eat at all, because none of the kids will give you money for food. They'd rather give you drugs than give you money for food, 'cause they want all their money to go for drugs. To eat, I'd have to turn a trick like I did in the morning or else I just buy some drugs and don't bother eating at all. That's why all the kids you see be so skinny, 'cause they smoke that crack and don't ever bother eating. I used to be 180 pounds, now I'm what, 110? Some mornings I go to the Health Department to pick up some condoms, sometimes I go visit my doctor at The One. She's been really good to me, like a mother I never had. That's about it. Turning tricks, doing crack. Eating and sleeping when I can't go no more.

Discussion

Like Aptekar's (1988) *desamperados*, Tracy and other wounded street youths found "sustenance without cunning in shelters," and could "barely cope without relying on someone who could give them help" (p. 212).[27]

Pumps and Pearls

I have addressed transvestite culture separately because, as will become clear, this community is distinctly and uniquely fascinating. The songs *Walk on the Wild Side* (Reed, 1990) and *Lola* (Davies, 1977), and the movies *Cabaret* (Feuer & Fosse, 1972), *Victor/Victoria* (Edwards, 1982), and *Paris is Burning* (Livingston, 1990), capture different perspectives of transvestite culture in vivid form. Green (1993), Suggs (1988), and Pooley (1990) have provided social commentary with articles on Vogueing, Balls, and Houses. In observing these youths, I tried to "focus on the phenomenon of what they did when together" (Aptekar, 1988, p. 119). What follows is my attempt to convey the unique and engaging world of the City streets. At the behest of my member checkers, I have called this category *Pumps and Pearls*.

All of the transvestite youths I met in the field were Black or Hispanic, an observation consistent with Green's (1993), Pooley's (1990), and Suggs' (1988). My informants were from the metropolitan area and had grown up in poor or working class homes. Of some interest was the fact that several white and Hispanic gay youths I had known in my practice and two of my informants had been engaged in the transvestite lifestyle as younger adolescents, but had matured to express a "butch" or gay male-identified sexual orientation.

Several qualities characterized the transvestite youths of my acquaintance. Humor, creativity, a highly developed sense of irony, and a playful attitude toward language were evident in generous measure. Theatricality and dramatization were prominent. These attributes as a whole define the gay concept of *camp*. Finally, a charged sexuality was palpable in the presence of these youths. In all these attributes the quality of competitiveness was present, hence the theme, "Anything you can do, I can do better." These qualities will be discussed individually, then I will attempt an assay of the impact of these qualities taken as a whole. A discussion of Houses, Balls, and Vogueing follows in the subtheme, The Elements of Vogue.

Humor and Language

Observing these youths required that I maintain mental agility and alertness, no easy task at one in the morning. The youths spoke rapidly with a patois I had heard in my work at the Center, part Latin, part Jamaican, and part City, but much of their language was new to me. I frame this linguistic distancing in the theme, "I can use your words so you don't know what they mean." Some examples follow, with approximate translations.

"Those bamboos are fierce, child." [Those heavy hoop earrings are awesome.]

"I'm going to call Bessie later and find out what's shing-a-linging." [I'm going to call Bessie later and find out what's happening.]

"I don't know why you want to invite them to the party, you know they'll get there late, and smoke some jumbos and kiki and fool around, and then it will be time to go, so what's the significance of that?" [they'll get there late and smoke some large marijuana cigarettes and giggle a lot and fool around. . .]

[Of a youth with a black eye,] "She got japped is what happened to her." [She got punched is what happened to her.]

"Look at them, they're bourging." [Look at them, they're trying to act bourgeois.]

"She's got junk in her trunk." [She's crazy.]

On one occasion, I was talking with Jay, a veteran of Special Education and an early dropout, and he regaled me with his slow and expressive tale of a stolen date book, notable for its use of language and drama.

I was walking over to the bank this morning and some guy called in my wallet. No, not my wallet, my date book. It only had five dollars in it, that's all I'd ever carry in there, and he snagged me, he called it in. He'll be so wounded when he sees there's only five dollars in it, but that's all he's getting. My wallet and my bank card were in another pocket. Oh, but my phone numbers. I guess my friends will be in for a surprise! (Jay, Log, p.78.39-50)

Conversations were sprinkled with "Miss Thing," an appellation deriving from Count Basie's (1972) instrumental of the same name, which paid homage to a female impersonator. The term as used by my respondents connoted both scorn and admiration.

Aptekar (1988) noted that the private language of his informants might occasionally be shared with a trusted other. The "secret code" he observed was a way the children had to express group and self-definition and to mark the boundary between themselves and outsiders. This was clearly the case with my informants, as they seemed to vaunt their streetwise fluency to outsiders. Only when I was well acquainted with them did I risk seeking understanding and was gratified that they shared their special argot with me.

Humor was quick and often acerbic, expressed in the theme, "Child, I can make you laugh 'til you cry." On one occasion, a girl responded, "Don't call me Miss Thing. I'm not missing anything" (Unidentified, Log, p. 28.13-15). Another girl, trying to board the van on the heels of another, said, "Girrrul, if you don't get out of my way, I am going to pull every hair right out your ass" (Unidentified, Log, p. 28.18-21). A subsequent interchange demonstrated not only humor but literacy—"Child, look at that hair. She teased it and then she overteased it." "Yeah, and what about you? You the Black Medusa?" (Karena & Tina, Log, p. 28.22-26). I have cited in a previous section an exchange Solotaroff (1990) documented with respect to a youth's evasiveness—"I can skate alright. I'm the Black Dorothy Hamill!" (p. 36).

Although a few straight youths floated rare humorous comments, this degree of humor was unique to the transvestite and gay youths. These youths were no less deprived or distressed than my straight informants; however, it seemed that the gay community expected and modeled a camp attitude among its proponents, whatever their circumstances. The ability to express camp was a source of status within the community. Companions to camp were the attitudes of *giving attitude* and *giving shade*, overt and subtle put-downs of competitors.

A Flair for Drama

My transvestite informants were single-minded in their pursuit of the theatrical, no subject too common, no audience too small. This propensity was reflected in their dress, their demeanor, their conversation, and the fluidity of their roles, and in the theme, "I am such a star." On one evening "the girls" were dressed outrageously in leather jackets, short skirts, and sported long red fingernails and hair out to here! On other nights, I saw formfitting neon bright dresses, bustiers and brassieres, prim skirts and blouses, and lycra leggings, tops, and skirts. Spiked high heels, the pumps of *Pumps and Pearls*, were de rigueur, which occasioned this conversation:

> I would like to know, Rhonda, how you walk in those. I can't even walk on 2" heels! [Rhonda, sliding off a 6" heeled pump] 'It's easy, child, you just put them on [replacing shoe] and walk!' (Katherine & Rhonda, Log, p. 35.1-7).

On another evening, the same question elicited a different response from the assembled femmes—"Practice!" (Chorus, Log, p. 56.22).

The girls changed attitudes as frequently as they changed clothes, variously appearing as quiet and sedate, vivacious and outgoing, or reticent and dignified. Hair color and styles, attire, and even bust size were observed to change with persona, such that it was often a challenge to recognize the youths from week to week.

I commented in my field notes that the movements of the youths were exaggerated,[28] observing on one occasion two transvestite youths glide up to the van, open the door, and enter imperiously, as if it were their personal limousine. A common activity saw the youths mimicking commercials or weaving the illusion of an elegant cocktail party. "Could you pass the Gray Poupon?," an illusion to the high concept media campaign for Gray Poupon® mustard, was a line I heard repeated almost daily, at the Center, on the van, and on the streets. Upon entering the van and taking seats, one or another youth would invariably start the charade—"Oh, could you pass the pate? And could I get a glass of wine?" I entered the spirit of the occasion, offering KoolAid® I identified as Pouilly-Fuisse®. Then all assumed the game and would ask for smoked salmon as I distributed sandwiches or allow, "Oh no, I wanted the Belgian caviar." Affected posturing and intonation accompanied the conversation, with the youths lifting shoulders and dropping wrists to accentuate their dialogue. Even cigarettes became props, as they smoked in the manner of twenties flappers.

Green (1993)[29] noted the theatricality his informants demonstrated: "looking like endangered birds, the drag queens, tottered on their heels as they entered—'a bit early in the day for we girls,' one said" (p. 11, Section 9).

Gender Bending

The projection of the themes, "I am sexual, I am fierce" and "Sex is my life" were predominantly observed in the transvestite gay male population. The overtly erotic sexuality of the transvestite kids was communicated by provocative attire, intense eye contact, seductive body movement, self-stroking and caressing, erotic touching of other youths, and innuendo or straightforward suggestion. These behaviors, when observed in nontransvestite youths, were usually in the context of prostitution.

These youths were very concerned with creating an illusion of femininity and competed intensely with one another in this respect. The primacy of this pursuit is suggested by the theme, "I am a *real* girl." Livingston (1990) and Suggs (1988) cited Realness as being of great import to transvestite ball entrants, sometimes to a point approaching delusion. Realness was, in fact, the chief criterion for judging competitions and Ball categories carried such appellations as "Schoolgirl Realness" and "Movie Star Realness." The quest for realness was reflected in several interchanges I observed. Of Natalia, one girl said, "She's on hormones, that Miss Thing. Not me, girrul. My breasts are the real thing. I'm a real girl" (Unidentified, Log, p. 36.16-19). Later, as the girls departed the van, Tina, or was it Rhonda, said, "Did you see that girl? What an actor." Caressing herself, she added, "Not me, honey. I'm a real girl" (Unidentified, Log, p. 36.15-20). In counterpoint, drag performer Dorian Corey disclaimed to Green (1993), as he donned four inch rhinestone earrings, "I'm not trying to look real" (Section 9, p. 11). The girls were in fact well endowed, their assets effected through strategically placed padding, hormone therapy, and implants.[30] Desiree, commenting that she was "just out here working to pay for [breast] implants," was told by a straight peer, "You've got plenty. What you want more for?" and responded, "It's not enough. I just want more" (Desiree and Vance, Log, p. 79.12-16). Many of the girls were exquisitely beautiful, an observation not lost on outreach staff, who commented with admiration and wonder on particular girls.

Transvestite youths appropriated or simulated another act usually practiced by females. Birk and other youths instructed me that *douching* referred to an enema administered by the youths for hygienic and symbolic purposes prior to engaging in anal receptive intercourse (personal conversations, 1988–1990), a practice my concerned instruction did little to discourage.

Maximum Impact

If humor, drama, and hypersexuality defined the group experience of my transvestite informants, the combined effect of these qualities on an observer was powerful. The interaction of individuals and qualities converged to create a synergistic effect, such that the total impact of the group was that of a single organism engaged in a complex choreography of sight and sound. This effect was confounded by the sense of dislocation which I, as a straight and somewhat naive woman, experienced when I tried to reconcile what I saw, girls, with what I thought I knew, boys. I first experienced this sense of confusion when I cared for a transvestite youth at the Center. Though I knew Josie was male and s\he was wearing pants and a sweater, the feminine comportment, curly ponytail, and light makeup over her finely freckled face identified her as female, and I found myself provoked and somewhat anxious. A similar feeling developed when I met Alia. She wore a simple flowered blouse and soft cotton trousers. "Aha," I thought, "a genotypic female!" noting her delicate skin and soft demeanor. I did not learn until later that Alia was in fact a boy. As I contemplated this revelation, I felt my sense of order in the world go topsy turvy. Such was my experience of the assembled transvestite kids. As Davies (1977) wrote in *Lola*, "Girls will be boys and boys will be girls, it's a mixed up world, it's a shook up world, except for Lola."

Aptekar (1988) indicated that the researcher's responses to informants may yield valuable insights into the nature of the observed phenomena. I realized as I reflected on my reactions to these youths that they violated most of the dominant society's taboos regarding sexual behavior. In appropriating the forbidden, these youths aroused in me and other outsiders a sense of hubris or "id consciousness," as it were. The dissonance this perception provoked among mainstream observers generally required that the observer reject the source of discomfort to avoid further disorganization. Fortunately with respect to my research, my fascination with these youths surpassed my discomfort. I believe that this observation explains the extremely hostile responses straight kids manifested toward the youths and the negative sanctions society imposed on them.[31]

The Elements of Vogue

My awareness of *vogueing* developed as I worked at the Center and observed many gay youths engaging in a peculiar combination of 'freeze frame' poses and flowing movement—

> lightning-fast hand motions and whirling arms, swoops and spins on the ground, and improbable contortions, all delivered with an elegant deadpan attitude. (Pooley, 1990, p. 56)

Upon further inquiry, I learned vogueing was named after the fashion magazine and evolved from the Harlem Balls at which drag queens emulated celebrated runway models.

That vogueing and its associated social networks were important to the gay youths was evident in the frequent allusions I heard to the practice.

> 'Are you vogueing?' 'Not this time.' 'Are you?' 'Yes, but I'm not competing.' 'Are you going to vogue?' 'No, child, I'm not going to that ball. They aren't going to make me walk with those B-Q[32] girls.' 'You don't want to walk [compete]?' (Unidentified, Log, p. 28.30-33, 53-54 and p. 29.1-2)

One evening, I observed one youth, Felicia, vogueing in silence for a long period, as *house music* pounded from the van's radio. She was in a trance-like state for twenty minutes or more, swaying and vogueing. At length, I asked her what she thought about when she vogued. "Oh," she replied after a long pause, "I just listen to the music" (Felicia, Log, p. 29.25-26). On another occasion, I watched Darlene and Christa vogueing in a back seat, turning frequently to look at one another with a 'freeze frame' pose, still and staring as if for a camera, then dissolving into giggling.

In his article on balls and houses, Pooley (1990) concluded that vogueing fulfilled several functions—it served as entertainment, an art form, a source of identification and affiliation, and as an expression of contempt for the ruling classes—"a nice polite way to say 'fuck you' to the people in charge" (p. 110). Suggs (1988) indicated that accomplishment at vogueing was a source of self-esteem to gay youths who in other company met disapprobation.

Vogueing did not propagate in isolation, but developed in the context of Houses and Balls. According to Suggs (1988), the "dozen or so Houses active in today's Ball scene grew out of the transvestite community that patronized the costume balls of the early to mid sixties" (p. 28). A House was, according to Pooley (1990), a "dance and fashion clique" comprised of 20 to 75 members. The group joined ostensibly to provide a forum and support for ball competitions, but in practice assumed a surrogate family role for many youths whose families ostracized them because of their gay identification. Suggs quoted Willie:

> Some people think a House is just a place to hang out, but it's also a financial partnership, a creative partnership, and an emotional partnership. A lot of the ball kids don't have families who take care of them, so they join a house. (p. 25)

Green (1993) elaborates:

> As mother of the House of Xtravaganza, Angie had taken in many rejected, wayward, even homeless children; had fed them, observed their birthdays; taught them all about 'walking the balls'. (p. 11, Section 9)

Suggs likewise confirmed this, stating that the Houses "also served to formalize the values and relationships that sustained their members" (p. 27).

Each House had a parent, who was called mother if a *femme queen* and father if a *butch queen*. The parent was an older gay, experienced and accomplished in the way of the transvestite culture. The parent's role was to counsel the youths about their outfits and strategies for winning competitions, but the House parent also assumed a nurturing, mentoring role toward the youths.

Suggs (1988) quoted *Princess Myra*, a female denizen of the ball circuit, on the House and Ball phenomenon:

> They had their own star system. These aren't people who are normally accepted in the real world. So they have to create a world where they can be praised. Everybody needs praise and adulation. (p. 23)

In effect, the Houses and Ball competitions served several functions. Explicitly, the Houses existed to host and support the Ball competitions. The Balls provided a showcase for performance artists who emerged in a marginal subculture and allowed those individuals, "members of a despised double minority—both ethnic and sexual" (Ansen, 1991), the illusion of possessing a world from which they were excluded; "the victory of imagination over poverty" (Green, 1993, Section 9, p. 11). Implicit in the Houses' purposes were communicating and perpetuating vogueing as a cultural expression and an art form, nurturing and sustaining transvestite gay youths, and socializing gay Black and Latino youths to the transvestite lifestyle.

Notes

1. A woman crack user who is to be used for sex and then "tossed" away; Goldsmith, 1993. This phenomenon is discussed at length in the Crack House section; see pp. 86, 130.

2. Similarly in Kennedy et al., 1990.

3. Similarly in Louie, p. 4.21-23.

4. Similarly in Yancey, 1992.

5. Street argot for the stimulant drug methamphetamine.

6. Similarly in Goldsmith, 1993; and Weisberg, 1985.

7. Street argot for transvestite.

8. Similarly in Weisberg, 1985.

9. Similarly in Goldsmith, 1993; and Solotaroff, 1990.

10. Similarly in Visano, 1991.

11. Similarly in McMullen, 1986; V. Price, 1989; and Saltonstall, 1984.

12. Similarly in Deborah, audiotape.

13. Similarly in Goldsmith, 1993.

14. Similarly in V. Price, 1989.

15. Similarly in Chiauzzi, 1991.

16. Similarly in Cates and Markley, 1992.

17. Similarly in my interview with Junior.

18. Similarly in Livingston, 1990.

19. See Pumps and Pearls, p. 84, 115, 154, 158, 166, 173, 84.

20. See Pumps and Pearls, p. 84, 115, 154, 158, 166, 173, 84.

21. Similarly in Visano, 1991.

22. Similarly in Goldsmith; and Solotaroff, 1990.

23. Similarly in Bollinger, 1988a, p. 22.

24. Similarly in Schaffer and DeBlassie, 1984.

25. Street argot for stealing.

26. Similarly in V. Price, 1989; and Wilkinson, 1987.

27. Similarly in Simon et al., 1992.

28. Similarly in Green, 1993; and Suggs, 1988.

29. Similarly in Solotaroff, 1990; and Suggs, 1988.

30. Also noted in "Device and Consent," 1992a.

31. Similarly in Elifson, Boles, Posey, Sweat, Darrow, and Elsea, 1993.

32. A derogatory comment impugning suburban or Brooklyn–Queens rivals.

VI

Public Masks and Private Faces: Core Categories and Themes

Introduction

In the chapter which follows, I address the research subquestion about the qualities, attitudes, and values my informants communicated. A cluster of related elements emerged with respect to qualities shared by my informants. I have called this dimension "Public Masks and Private Faces," in recognition of the vulnerable core I discerned beneath the bravado attitude youths presented to the public. This category encompasses the patterns identified in the self-perceptions and attitudes which the youths expressed, and in their hopes, aspirations, and illusions.

Sereny (1985) observed that her informants were "intelligent, imaginative, warm, curious, and loving" (p. 71), while Simon et al. (1992) indicated that their respondents were "calm, cooperative, insightful, and extremely open" (p. 36). These qualities should be borne in mind as the reader considers other attributes of street kids noted in the following paragraphs.

Outlaw

As I listened to my respondents telling about jumping turnstiles, stiffing taxis, snagging or mopping goods and currency, and noted their engagement in prostitution, procurement, drug dealing and extreme drug use, it became apparent that in these activities, the youths demonstrated a disregard for authority and a disdain for the norms of the dominant culture. The *Maverick* or *Outlaw* persona was expressed in the themes "I do what I want," "I live by my own rules," "I do what I have to do."

One youth told this story about Rocco: "I saw Rocco, yeah. Ah, man, he was leaving the Pagoda and he and another guy decide they're going to snatch some lady's purse. So they tried, but she wouldn't let go of it, and people started hitting them and shit, and they got arrested and thrown in jail" (Chris, Log. p. 22.41-50 and p. 21.1-2).

Sarah, in jail "too many times to be counting" (Sarah, p. 10.14), likewise professed nonconformity, having been arrested for "everything they could catch me of. Carrying controlled substances, as the stuff, a jumbo, uh, trying to make a sale or prostitution, right. You know, all that good stuff" (Sarah, p. 11.2-6). Having taken her first lover at nine, she said of her free lifestyle, "Religious people call it sinning, other people call it fornication, but I call it fun" (Sarah, p. 20.2-3). As the youngest and only female member of a gang, she was tattooed, "fucked up every cop that came near us" (Sarah, p. 25.15), and with her compeers, waged gang warfare.

Louie, veteran of many years of incarceration, drug use, hustling, and street life describes his transition to outlaw and his present involvement:

> I was like in the corner all my life. I never had anybody I could talk to. So I started getting more aggressive as I got older, more meaner, more cold shouldered. At 14, I got busted (Louie, p. 8.28-32). I love to rip off necklaces, gold. I steal, 'cause they got a lot of money, so I take it. They don't like it, what are they gonna do? They can't do nothing. They are coming

out picking somebody up, coming to town to get their
dicks sucked, well, that's not all you get (Louie,
p. 20.27-34 and p. 21.1-2). So I just give them a
warning, "Stay away." That's all (Louie, p. 21.8-9). I've
pimped off lots of boys (Louie, p. 24.9). They're out
there anyways trying to sell themselves so why don't I
do them a favor. I'm helping them out. (Louie,
p. 24.33-35)

Many sources document the parallels of background and
lifestyles observed in delinquent and homeless youths. The
neglect, abuse, and family conflict; poor school performance,
drug use, and asocial behaviors; the institutionalization,
incarceration, and alienation that characterize homeless youths
are virtually indistinguishable from the life histories of their
delinquent counterparts (Calhoun, Jurgens, & Chen, 1993;
Clark, 1992; Feitel et al., 1992; Hagan & McCarthy, 1992;
McCarthy & Hagan, 1992; Yancey, 1992). The only significant
difference, according to Hagan and McCarthy, in delinquent
and homeless youths is that delinquent activities accelerated
after youths left home.

Calhoun et al. (1993) and Pagnozzi (1994) indicated that
the incidence and nature of criminal activity among females has
intensified in the past decade. "They carry blades in their
cheeks, knives in their pony tails, guns in their bras. And they
use them. The girls they got hard. And nobody knows how it
happened" (Pagnozzi, p. 122).

By engaging in delinquent behaviors such as those described
above, street youths "lose the tolerance adult society usually
affords its juveniles, and the youths become perceived of as
dangerous and deviant" (Kennedy et al., 1990, p. 87), dynamics
which reinforced the youths' sense of alienation. Visano (1991)
speculated that "the subterranean values of the street culture

act as a defense mechanism which protects [youths] from the negative attitudes of outsiders around them" (p. 204).

The Outlaw has its rough parallel in the *gamine* lifestyle described by Aptekar (1988). The *gamines* were children who were socialized by their poor families for early independence. Their public posture was one of nonconformity and disdain for more conservative types. Aptekar wrote that the street skills of daring, physical dexterity, haughtiness, and a public display of disregard for authority defined the *gamine*. Through rules, poses, and attitude, the *gamine* was socialized to the streets. Though many similarities obtain, the Outlaw differs from the *gamine* in that whereas the *gamines* were motivated by mischief, the Outlaw youths tended to be less spirited and more emotionally injured than the *gamines* (Aptekar, p. xiii), and more harsh as predators.

Born to Die

A pervasive spirit of futility and nihilism was evident among my informants, an observation I have called "Born to Die." This category is represented by the theme "I've got nothing to live for." This hopelessness manifested itself in a variety of self-destructive behaviors—in overt and veiled suicide attempts, reckless sexual activity, a widespread refusal to use condoms, sharing needles, and most acutely, in getting high.[1]

Jon spoke poignantly of his despair: "Yeah, everybody says I seem really smart. But what's the use? I finished the ninth grade. I've done some carpentry, but I've got nothing to show for it. I feel sometimes like there's nothing for me to do but to finish killing myself" (Jon, Log, p. 66.12-17).

Tracy, a lovely tall Black girl of 21, had attempted suicide twice. She also spoke of her hopelessness:

> I don't worry about AIDS. Sometimes I think I
> have a death wish. I never thought I'd live this long
> (Tracy, p. 19.10-12). I feel hopeless. . . and alone. . . I
> like myself. It's just that nobody else does. (Tracy,
> p. 20.8-15)

Tracy's violent demise was noted in earlier chapters.

Pete, on the streets a year, had played soccer, ridden bikes, and engaged in other demanding competitive sports. "It was alright, I guess, but I like my smoke" (Pete, Log, p. 26.10-14). Asked if he would consider being tested for the AIDS virus, he shouted, "Hell yes! If I was negative, I'd quit this shit and go back home" (Pete, Log, p. 26.24-29).

An informant told Luna (1991), "I live on the street, I don't really have anyone. I die everyday. I'm not afraid of death, I'm afraid of life" (p. 513).[2]

In their despair, my informants, focusing on their inner pain, seemed unable to assume mastery of their circumstances. This dynamic, like that of "feeling different," prevented their assimilation into the workaday world and perpetuated their isolation.

Aptekar (1988) identified three types of street children in Colombia—the *gamines* who evinced joy and mischief in their lifestyles, the *desamperados* who were coping marginally, and the *chupagruesos* who were needy, vulnerable, and poorly adjusted. He indicated that the "emotionally injured runaways of North America" were most like the Colombian *chupagruesos*, lacking confidence, humor, and spirit (p. 212).[3]

True Blue

Several youths spoke of their regard for human life—all except their own, that is—and other kids reflected this attitude in their behavior. I have articulated this belief in the theme, "I care about others but not myself." Two youths manifested this quality in ways affecting even to hardened workers—Joni, a transvestite, was seen cruising Cannery Row on a bitterly cold and windy night, when even her peers were warmly dressed, wearing heels, stockings, a garter belt, and a nylon windbreaker. I remembered Karl's words—"It's cold outside, you be smoking that crack, you aren't cold long. Everybody else is freezing, you be peeling off your clothes" (Karl, Log, p. 56.48-54 and 49.1-2).

Wanda, a hefty young woman with a sallow complexion, few teeth, and a swollen jaw, related as she solicited tricks, many of whom would require fellatio, that "I went to the dentist yesterday and he pulled my tooth. But I think he hurt me, I think I've got an abscess now" (Wanda, Log, p. 49.3-9). Upon hearing this, a long silence ensued, as the usually gregarious staffers pondered her words. Overwhelmed, Jeff whispered, "Pitiful what a rough world this is" (Jeff, Log, p. 49.24) and we drove on, unable to tolerate the chasm of her need.

The youths recognized the contradiction inherent in caring for others but not themselves, but were unable to effect a change:

> I guess I'm not the kind of person to do those things [stealing, dealing]. I think it's wrong. I would just never do that. What I'm doing hurts only myself. (Jon, Log, p. 66.4-7)

Anyway, I danced in front of men. It was like, uh, demoralizing yourself. It was against my upbringing, it was against my own morals, but it was something that I could do without hurting anybody else. I'm not the type of person to go around robbing somebody, if you know what I mean. I mean, I could barely hurt a fly, you know, I say that I love life so much that I couldn't hurt another human being, but I hurt myself so much. (Rick, p. 2.7-16)

Solotaroff (1990), noting that most street kids would sell their bodies before they would sell crack, suggested that "dealing is an act of violence against other people; hustling your body to men who won't wear condoms is an act of violence against yourself, a carrying out of the sentence handed down in childhood" (p. 36).

Sexual Feeling

Though the concern of street kids' sexuality as distinct from prostitution emerged late in my analysis I cite it as a minority theme articulated as "Smoking crack turns me on." Allusions to sexuality were made with respect to the effect of crack on sexual expression. Transvestite sexuality is discussed in Pumps and Pearls, but the phenomenon of hypersexuality is believed to obtain with respect to crack users generally. One youth commented on her experience of sex under the influence of cocaine:

When you smoke, it's just like somebody when they're drunk—they can't get it up [get an erection]. It's the same with these guys, only it's worse, because all they want to do is smoke more crack. Their mind is saying "Let's do this," [have sex], but their body is saying, "No, get away from me!" So the guys want to have sex and the girls want to smoke, so that's what

they [the girls] have to do [accommodate the guys].
(Tracy, p. 25.6-16)

Peter, a street kid, told Solotaroff (1990):

I'm a pretty normal person. I wouldn't consider
myself a sex fiend. But when I'm on that pipe, all I can
think about—bang—is fucking. Fucking, smoking, and
fucking some more. And I'll tell you what, when that
head [feeling] comes over me, I gotta go somewhere
quick and beat my meat, or I'm liable to kill someone.
(p. 37)

This feeling of enhanced desire or hypersexuality associated
with crack use was also noted by Weiss (personal conversation
with Kerr, 1989), a drug treatment expert and psychiatrist at
Cornell University. With large doses of cocaine or crack, users
are sexually aroused but cannot achieve orgasm; they may
engage in sexual intercourse or masturbation for hours, often
with many partners.[4] In addition, women in crack houses often
exchange sex for drugs. Kennedy et al. (1990), Kerr (1989);
and Schwarcz et al. (1991) cautioned that this effect is of
major public health concern in that crack driven hypersexuality
in the acutely high-risk population of street kids is a critical
vector of syphilis, hepatitis, gonorrhea, and the human
immunodeficiency virus.

Other researchers challenge the notion of crack induced
hypersexuality, indicating that in many individuals, crack
suppresses desire (Goldstein, 1992; Fagan & Chin, 1991;
Weatherby et al., 1992). As one informant proclaimed to
Goldstein, "A rockhead don't have no sex drive" (p. 358).

Most researchers investigating street youths acknowledged
that the youths were sexually active and often engaged in
prostitution, but only a few had examined the phenomenon of

the youths' sexuality. Moya (cited in Bond et al., 1992) indicated that street youth engaged in transactional sex for money or goods; comfort sex, typfied by affection and consideration, and recreational sex, characterized by the relief of sexual tension. Other researchers (Brown, 1979; Cavaiola & Schiff, 1988; Silbert & Pines, 1983) concluded that these youths might be eroticized as a result of early sexual stimulation and abuse. In contrast, Aptekar (1988) made little reference to the sexuality of his informants. He indicated that youthful female prostitutes occupied a niche in society separate from street youths, and that girls, living with their families, were peripheral to his study. He argued that homosexual activity was rare among the boys because it would require a surrender of autonomy which was antithetical to the *gamine* lifestyle and might compromise their positions within the *gallada*.

Going Straight

The theme "I'm getting off the streets someday," of anticipating and planning for a future, was evident in the hopes and thoughts of many youths, in contrapoint to the previous category, Born to Die. Heriberto's good fortune, the possibility of a professional dance career, was noted previously. Alia, a beautiful transvestite youth, told me she was in the Eleventh grade, living with her parents, and was eager to finish school and go on to college, "Out of state," she allowed (Alia, Log, p. 35.18-19). Other youths remarked on their intentions:

> You will not be seeing me for long, I'm going back to school next month. I was in school before. I'm not like the rest of these drug users. I'm just out here working for my [breast] implants. (Desiree, Log, p. 97.8-13)

This is it. I am going to make a life. I'm going to get in a drug program for two years. I'm tired of this shit. (Angela, Log, p. 80.4-7)

I have just had enough. You just get to the point where it's too much. What you're doing to yourself, what you let other people do to you. You just have to go through it 'til you get sick of it. (Group discourse, Log, p. 80.35-40)

I want to get a full-time job and get off the streets. (Darryl, p. 19.1-2) I work, but I never sold my body and took drugs and sold drugs. You know there's too much to live for. (Darryl, p. 13.15-17)

Junior alone expressed his ambivalence about leaving the streets, perhaps related to his fear of failure:

Familiarity. It's all I know. . . I shouldn't say that it's all I've known, because I have known better and I have done better. But yet, you know people out there and you know how malicious and how evil they can be or selfish, but you tend not to think about that, you think about the fun. (Junior, p. 26.15-22 and p. 27.1-3)

When a person is so used to living a life in the streets for so long, it's very difficult for them to go back. Because when they've done something for so long that they're used to it, anything else is alien, it's different. You know, it doesn't seem right. You, you're used to doing something for so long and that's just what you want to keep doing. (Junior, p. 8.15-21 and p. 9.1-5)

Cassie told Sereny (1985) "I don't like to think about tomorrow. I just take every day as it comes" (p. 78).

My sense is that my informants intuited at some level that their chances for getting off the streets alive were marginal. The former passages suggest to me a mechanism that might have enabled the youths, through a deliberately created illusion, to persevere in the face of extreme hardship.

Earlier studies by Weisberg (1985) and Sereny (1985) indicated that several of their respondents left the streets, seemingly without difficulty. In contrast, Goldsmith (1993) quotes Joyce Wallace, an investigator of AIDS in prostitutes:

> These women represent the failures of our society. They are the products of two decades of inadequate schools, dysfunctional families, domestic violence, and incest, problems that may be irreparable. (p. 66, 81)

Aptekar (1988) indicated that in Colombia, adolescence represented a period of transition between the mischief of street children and the choices the youths made as they approached adulthood. Some youths would be able to enter the mainstream as steady workers, a few nonconformists would find a niche in the urban subculture of poverty that would support them. The remainder, the emotionally unfit, the alcoholics, the psychologically impaired, and the delinquents would remain on the fringes of adult society.

It is of interest that Junior, who expressed the most realistic appraisal of his street status, is the only one of my informants who has left the streets. Junior was an attractive and intelligent young man who possessed social savvy, reasonable insight, and a realistic appraisal of his abilities. He was able to commandeer and utilize needed resources from his environment, which included a caring benefactor, agency staff members who were invested in his well-being, and a few nonstreet peer contacts. He was able further to turn his skill and knowledge of the streets to his advantage as an AIDS peer counselor, from which he derived affiliation and self-esteem. Two other youths are believed to be in residential treatment centers and one is said to be in jail.

Saving Face

As I reflected on my field notes, I observed that several youths manifested a pattern of exaggeration, evasion, and fabrication in the personas they presented to the public. I have called this category "saving face", expressed in the themes, "I can't bear to face the truth about myself" and "I can't let you see my frailty."

Jenny was observed to refuse our offer of sandwiches and KoolAid® , which a staff member attributed to her pride. One youth told Kerry, in contradiction to what we saw, that "I just come down here to the Wharf to see you" (Melvin, Log, p. 59.43-44). Pete, hungry and forlorn, advised us he "was staying uptown with friends" (Pete, Log, p. 26.50-51) and accepted food reluctantly.

Chris, in a moment of absolute denial, informed me even as he hustled tricks on the Circle, that "I hate needles. And I am very selective, real picky. I've only been with about ten girls in my life and they are clean!" (Chris, Log, p. 23.31-36). Joey told us, meeting the van on the Wharf, "I'm just down here looking for my boyfriend. I dumped him last week and oh, how he's suffering" (Joey, Log, p. 18.31-35). I came to believe that Jon's story of his architect girlfriend and a house in Park Slope and Louie's claim of frequent contact with his girlfriend and their child were confabulations offered to bolster their images in the eyes of outreach staff and myself.

Solotaroff (1990) confronted one youth about his evasiveness and the youth, Diego, admitted, "Oh, I can skate alright. I'm the Black Dorothy Hamill" (p. 36). Solotaroff made note of other youths telling an outreach worker, "Veronica, didja hear? I'm going away to college." "Veronica, Herbie told you we found this fly spot [room] in Rego Park?" (p. 37). He watched as the outreach worker listened to the youths, "treading delicately around their claims, knowing that was all they had" (p. 37).

Sereny (1985) observed that for street kids, "fantasy often equals energy, and the truth fatigue" (p. 88). "In their efforts to justify the lie they are living, to themselves more than to others, these children often spin a web of fantasies" (p. 39).

Aptekar (1988) indicated that Colombian street children possessed a highly practiced ability to observe their observers, manipulating information to their advantage (p. 15). They used this skill "to express and defend themselves, to make fun of the questioner, to evade or distance, and to get back at a society that devalued them" (p. 15). I believe this pattern of dissimulation may have represented the youths' efforts to defend themselves against exposure, to guard against emptiness, and to create the illusion of a brighter reality. Many of the aspirations youths depicted in the theme Going Straight might also be seen as saving face, a denial of and defense against the harsh reality of their lives.

Humor: No Fun Intended

Humor was a rare commodity in my informants, the exceptions being the gay and transvestite kids. This unequal balance of humor and gravity is expressed in the theme, "I don't have the resources to be funny." Nevertheless, my informants were capable of an occasional light comment. Deborah regularly announced herself with the line, "What's shaking, bacon?" One straight young man, always somber, told me one day that a cop had stopped him one day and inquired, "Are you James Edward Jenkins? I have a warrant with your name on it." He called me a few days later from a well known prison and announced with some irony that he was "at a Rehab Center in Queens" (Random Field Notes). Another youth, upon learning that I was a nurse, reported to me he had a pain in his back and inquired what I thought. His companion, Ronnie, miles ahead of me, responded, alluding to Chris's heroin addiction, "You've got a monkey on your back" (Log, p. 20.23-27). Darryl, a tense and angry young man, nevertheless was able to remark wryly that "I wasn't able to get disability, because those workers down there want more proof that I'm a mentally disturbed deranged young man" (Darryl, Log, p. 12.18-19).

Aptekar (1988) noted a sense of mischief and mirth among his informants, such as that elicited when the children hitched rides on car bumpers, but he did not identify humor specifically as characteristic of the children. Sereny (1985) noted that many of her informants "had a sense of humor, albeit a grim one" (p. 38). McGhee (1971) indicated that the sense of humor is a developmental phenomenon predicated on mastery of the environment, a competency sorely lacking in many of my informants. Burbridge (1978) observed that "people overwhelmed by problems do not readily laugh at them" (p. 11). Such was the case with many of my informants, whose difficult lives presented little occasion for humor.

I'm Running on Empty

On the streets, my informants manifested boredom, restlessness, and frequent changes, a pattern I have articulated in the theme "I'm just passing through." I have called the category "I'm Running on Empty" to convey a sense of restless movement driven by anxiety and emptiness, a quality I observed universally in my informants.

Weisberg (1985) noted "perhaps as a result of his chaotic early life, Bobby found it difficult to stay in any locale for any length of time" (p. 24). Gabriel (1992), speaking of the youthful lover of a business tycoon, noted that "S.R. was restless and periodically disappeared for weeks" (p. 60). Some youths drifted from trick to trick, staying with dates for days, weeks, or even months, moving when "the thing crapped out over drugs or house rules" (Solotaroff, 1990, p. 36).[5] Others stayed with family members, friends, or in cheap hotel rooms, decamping when things got tight or a new venture beckoned. A number of youths reported frequent travel, sometimes with tricks, at other times making the rounds of runaway shelters in distant communities. Sarah would catch a bus to Florida,

> fifty-nine dollars for a two day ride. I get myself a job up there plus at night I work the streets (Sarah, p. 24.11-13). But when I get to missing the City, I come back. (Sarah, p. 24.19)

Bo entered a drug program, but couldn't tolerate being inside the same place for more than a few days and left. "I just couldn't handle it. The walls were closing in on me" (Bo, Log, p. 80.1). Pete had a similar experience—"I was bugging," he recalled (Pete, Log, p. 23.44):

> I just got to get out! It's so boring!!! I'm on the streets, oh, a year, a year and a half. I was so bored at home. Nothing to do, boring. I used to run away for a couple of days at a time, just for something to do. Then I came here for some excitement, tried that crack, and that was it. I want to get help, but nothing seems to work. [You don't feel lonely or hurting?] No, just bored. (Pete, Log, p. 23.48-54, p. 24.1-6)

Other youths demonstrated some insight into this pattern, describing their restlessness as a longstanding phenomenon:

My mom left when I was three and she left with my biological sister, who was two months and we were raised with but they took my sister real quick, and me, I was shifted. That's why I have this shifting pattern going here and going there 'cause from like three to seven I was shifted from one family to the next family to this part of the family to that part of the family with different aunts and uncles. (Rocco, p. 2.6-20)

When I'm not motivated, if I go into a program, I don't really do anything. I'm just sitting in one spot, you know. And that makes me crazy, like I wanna get out, it's like being locked up.   (Tracy, p. 28.34-35, p. 29.1-3)

I've been homeless like since I was 16, what's that, uh, seven years, six years. In and out of places, I, I can't say that I was truly homeless, you know, I was like uh, stayed here for six months, meaning uh, here and there were tricks, you know. (Rick, p. 1.7-13)]

Morse et al. (1991) attributed the nomadic existence of their informants to four factors: "wanderlust, trouble with the law, unsettled scores on the streets, or because of the need to follow the tourist season in pursuit of prostitution's 'easy money' " (p. 538). His subjects, a group of male street prostitutes, covered travel expenses by trading or selling sex while on the road.

Liebow (1967) remarked of Black street corner men, "Transience is perhaps the most striking and pervasive characteristic of this street corner world" (p. 218), an observation consistent with my own observations of street youths. Aptekar (1988) observed that his informants "often traveled a great deal to other parts of the country for diversion" (p. 26). He argued against the prevailing sentiment that street children moved about aimlessly, stating on the contrary that their behavior exhibited "rational and functional qualities" (p. 115).

Upon examination of field notes and transcripts, I identified three forms of movement among street kids. These were the seemingly random flow of people and events around the youths, evidenced by their multiple placements, transient living arrangements, and fleeting friendships; the purposeful activity by which the youths secured food, clothing, pharmaceuticals, and other essential needs; and the restless driven movement Pete, Tracy, and Bo described in relation to their anomie. In the former case of externally imposed movement, the youths reminded me of tumbleweed, blown about and abraded by the currents of life. In the latter, internally driven movement, the youths were similar to Colombia's media depiction of street kids—"incessantly roaming, in a constant movement without direction" (Aptekar, 1988, p. 116). I believe that the ennui and restlessness street youths evinced and their inability to tolerate prolonged periods of introspection reflected the avoidance of pain and the absence of a meaningful inner life, consequences of the emotional deprivation of their early lives. This observation suggests that the excitement and stimulation of street life, coupled with the self-medication of drug use, provided my informants with relief from their gnawing emptiness and psychic pain.

Notes

1. Similarly in Goldsmith, 1993; and V. Price, 1989.

2. Similarly in LeBlanc, 1992; and Simon et al., 1992.

3. Rotheram-Borus, 1993, noted a high incidence of suicide attempts among street youths.

4. Similarly in Murphy and Rosenbaum, 1992; and Weatherby et al., 1992.

5. Similarly in Aptekar, 1988; Gabriel, 1992; and Morse et al., 1991.

VII

Conclusions and Recommendations

Conclusions

The present research encompassed a range of individuals and groups, attitudes and behavior, in a configuration which indicates the inherent diversity of street youths. The groups I had the opportunity to observe, male, female, and transvestite prostitutes, and one nonprostitute, complemented those Wilkinson (1987) studied, stoners and punk rockers. Safety considerations precluded my studying *punks*, whom outreach staff considered hostile and youths who, like Benjamin, lived in the innermost subterranean recesses of the City's surface transportation terminals. Research guidelines constrained me from studying minor youths, although many younger adolescents, including several as young as twelve and thirteen, were observed.

The question I sought to answer in the present research, "What are the lived experiences of a small group of street kids?" was addressed in considerable detail. The resources, social contacts, and life experiences of a small group of street youths were elaborated.

The present research enlarged on that of V. Price (1989), Sereny (1985), Weisberg (1985), and Wilkinson (1987) with respect to street youths engaged in prostitution. Aspects of the transvestite culture, certain of my informants' self-perceptions, and selected facets of street life suggested by popular literature but not previously documented were illumined. Other themes related to facets of street life and culture were identified and explored. These findings were compared and contrasted with those of Aptekar (1988), Wilkinson (1987), and other extant researchers as appropriate. In the following paragraphs, I propose a unifying theoretical construct descriptive of the life experiences of my informants.

On the Edge: A Descriptive Model of Street Youths

As I wrestled with the foregoing analysis in an attempt to articulate a descriptive model, I had the sudden realization that all of the themes and categories I had devised shared one common link—the lives of street kids unfolding "On the Edge." This quality was manifested in geographical, temporal, social, economic, and psychical realms.[1]

Youths existed literally on the periphery of society by frequenting isolated locations—abandoned areas of the City, hidden spaces in public buildings, and remote or inaccessible sites. Their nocturnal rhythms broke with prevailing patterns of the dominant culture, further separating the youths from mainstream society and engendering their associations with other marginal individuals. The solace these youths found in isolation led me to consider that this self-imposed seclusion represented a reenactment of the real abandonment the youths had experienced earlier.

Street youths elicited an ambivalent response in the mainstream culture. When such youths were portrayed sympathetically in the media, that is as mistreated and misunderstood children, or when a youth presented a pitiable appearance, as Jenny did, society's response was one of identification and concern. More often, however, the youths' engagement in nonnormative behaviors such as drug use, prostitution, and crime, elicited their rejection by the more conservative mainstream, which served to perpetuate the youths' isolation.

Absent a benefactor or generous date and lacking viable employment, my informants subsisted in a hand-to-mouth fashion, akin to the hunters and gatherers of primitive societies. Without resources, the youths, many of whom came from impoverished homes, sustained the divide between the haves and the have-nots, a social boundary of considerable import. With access to the mainstream thus obstructed, the youths again had the sense of outsiders looking in.

The normative developmental sequence saw major upheaval in street youths. Havighurst (1972) identified eight developmental tasks of adolescence, founded in large measure on Erik H. Erikson's (1982) elaboration of the adolescent struggle for identity. These tasks are listed below:

1. Trying on gender appropriate adult roles and experimenting socially within those roles,

2. Accepting and learning socially approved gender appropriate adult roles,

3. Accepting one's natural strengths and limitations and using those productively,

4. Achieving emotional independence of parents and other adults, while retaining mutual affection and respect,

5. Preparing for marriage and family life, including rearing children and home management,

6. Preparing for a viable career,

7.   Acquiring a set of values and an ethical system as a guide to behavior, and

8.   Desiring and achieving socially responsible behavior.

Thus, as their domiciled age-mates grappled with education, relationships, and the establishment of socially acceptable identities, street youths evinced attitudes and behaviors contrary to dominant social norms. In addition, they struggled with concerns their nonstreet peers took for granted—food, shelter, and clothing (V. Price, 1989), and warmth and safety (Aptekar, 1988). Aptekar further noted the decreased cognitive development and "diminished capacity to deal with the harshness of the streets" (p. 50) premature adolescence brought to this struggle.

Aptekar (1988) remarked of his informants that they were "young in age but old in experience" (p. 85).[2] In like manner, my informants demonstrated extreme precocity, having seen and endured experiences that remain foreign to most members of the dominant culture. This pattern reverberated in the youths' extreme loneliness, restlessness, and nihilism.

The urgency with which my informants pursued psychoactive drugs bespoke another extreme of experience. The youths sought through the use of mind-numbing drugs to escape unpleasant memories and to avoid present pain. The youths' self-destructive behaviors manifested a deeper conflict, having to do with the tension between life and death. V. Price (1989) indicated that with prolonged time on the streets, many youths become suicidal and others die "as a result of murder, overdose, or bizarre accidents" (p. 87). This conflict was epitomized in Paula's comment—"Who could blame me if I just took a bundle of heroin and never woke up again," and in Tracy's untimely death.

The idea of the descriptive formulation, On the Edge, derives support from several sources. Golden (1992) wrote *The Women Outside* with respect to homeless women. Homeless women engender dissonance among mainstream individuals because they lack homes and families, thus failing in the socially decreed female roles of homemaker and mother. Because such individuals violate certain assumptions about life that are essential to preserving the social order, society struggles to extinguish their effect, "the power of the formless to break down forms" (p. 217), through denial of their existence and denial of their common humanity. This distancing effects the marginalization seen in homeless women.

Scapegoating is another mechanism by which societies deal with deviant individuals (Golden, 1992). Formerly accomplished by ritual sacrifice, scapegoating presently assumes the form of unconscious projection. By attributing to outcasts what people inside society do not want to acknowledge in themselves and by expelling those outcasts, the community may preserve its integrity and ensure its survival (Golden, 1992).

These youths may also be seen to assume a protective role in our society in that they bear a disproportionate measure of society's violence, and provide a means for the expression of "deviant" sexual desire. By consigning street youths to the margin and by assigning them the function of scapegoat, society is able to externalize its evils and so preserve the status quo.

Balshem et al. (1992) relate the concept of stigma or deviance to the marginalization of street youths. Stigmatized individuals, according to Goffman,[3] possess an attribute that make them different from and less desirable from others not possessing that attribute.[4] Becker[5] states that social groups "create deviance by making the rules whose infraction constitutes deviance, and by applying those rules to particular people and labeling them as outsiders."[6] Ostracized groups may then seek to develop a distinct social identity by assuming symbols, meanings, and values in conflict with those of the dominant society (Ogbu, 1992).

Tait (1993) and C. Williams (1993) argue that labeling street youths as marginalized or as possessing a unique identifiable culture are divisive interventions, and mitigating against a more complete understanding of youths on the streets.[7] C. Williams suggests that the term *muted groups* more properly communicates the isolation and indifference such groups experience, and reframes the possibilities with respect to their effective assimilation.

Haley (1973) presented another conceptualization supportive of my On the Edge description of street youths. Drawing on the writings of Milton Erickson, Haley described the disturbed adolescent as a "peripheral animal." This metaphor, which I cite in its entirety, is uniquely descriptive of street kids:

> Among most animals, those who fail to establish a territory of their own during this crucial period [of adolescence] fall to the lowest status in the community and do not mate. They become peripheral animals, wandering about on the edges of the territory of others, and if they attempt to fight to gain space and status, they come up against the rule that the creature who controls space almost invariably wins when fighting on his own ground. These outcasts find that females are disinclined to mate with males who have not achieved status, and females who have not been selected as mates in turn become peripheral creatures, ignored by males and picked on by all females who have acquired mates and therefore status. The peripheral animals of most species are undefended and uncared for. They are

nature's discards, and are offered up to predators as part of the protection of the group. Their life is comparatively short, and they do not breed and reproduce their kind. (Haley, 1973, p. 46)

In summary, I have characterized street youths as possessing marginal status with respect to the dominant culture, their lives unfolding on the edge of society and experience. The peripheral position youths assumed expressed a mutual process as the isolation the youths sought was reflected in withdrawal by the mainstream. Marginalization of youths was argued to effect a protective mechanism for the dominant culture at the expense of the youths' welfare.

Recommendations

Certainly, there is ample direction within the field for further research. Many of the themes I identified would lend themselves to further study. In addition, I would recommend the following:

1. Examination of minor youths on the streets;

2. Exploration of the punk lifestyle;

3. Examination of those extraordinarily alienated youths who frequent the nearly impenetrable spaces of public buildings;

4. In-depth examination of the transvestite and house culture;

5. The prospective study of several youths over a period of years to explicate the influences which perpetuate or mitigate against the youths' staying on the streets;

6. A comparative study of intervention strategies designed to reclaim street youths; and

7. A qualitative study of youths in foster and group homes, focusing on supportive and destabilizing factors rather than the youths' dysfunction. Of particular interest might be a long-term prospective study of two uniquely deprived populations, those children of the "boarder baby" phenomenon which developed in the late '80s in response to the crack cocaine endemic in large cities, and those children orphaned by AIDS.

My findings make a strong case for more accessible drug rehabilitation targeted to the unique needs of street youths. Intensive and prolonged psychotherapy was suggested by V. Price (1989) and would surely facilitate the assimilation of some youths into the mainstream. Aptekar (1988) and C. Williams (1993) argue for the possibility of early access into adult status; this option too is predicated on the broader availability of viable vocational and educational choices. Researchers uniformly observe that street youths have negligible marketable job skills for legitimate employment and are excluded by bureaucratic constraints from vocational training and gainful employment (Balshem et al., 1992; Goldsmith, 1993; Murphy & Rosenbaum, 1992; Sereny, 1985; Pennbridge, et al., 1991).

Wurzbacher, Evans and Moore (1991) studied the effects of alternative schooling on youth involved in prostitution and concluded that "adolescents involved in street life and prostitution can benefit from services that encourage the acquisition of skills and promote competency" (p. 553). Rich (1990) reached a similar conclusion with respect to parenting skills in her study of homeless adolescent mothers.

Martin (1982) and Luna (1991) indicated that according the homeless the dignity and respect due them would diminish their isolation and facilitate their reintegration into the mainstream. Reform of the foster care and protective custody system is paramount, with the child's best interests rather than the family's right to self-determination of overriding concern.

Aptekar (1988) urged his readers to "reconsider the nature of children and how adult society is responsible for the well-being of those they choose to call children" (p. 211). I undertook this study in the belief that an enhanced understanding of street youths might provide new directions for research, suggest novel strategies for intervention, and foster the well-being of these wounded young people. I hope that in contemplating this material, the reader is challenged to consider how he or she might use this information to the advantage of other children and youths.

Notes

1. Similarly in Goldsmith, 1993; and Luna, 1991.

2. Similarly in C. Williams, 1993.

3. Cited in Balshem et al., 1992, p. 155.

4. Similarly in Balshem et al., 1992.

5. Cited in Balshem et al., 1992.

6. Similarly in Balshem et al., 1992.

7. Similarly in Aptekar, 1988.

Bibliography

Adams, G.R., Gullotta, T., & Clancy, M. (1985). Homeless adolescents: A descriptive study of similarities and differences between runaways and throwaways. Adolescence, 20, 715-724.

Adams, G.R. & Munro, G. (1979). Portrait of the North American runaway: A critical review. Journal of Youth and Adolescence, 8, 359-373.

Allen, M., Bonner, K., & Greenan, L. (1988). Federal legislative support for independent living. Child Welfare, 67(6), 515-527.

American Psychiatric Association. (1987). Diagnostic and statistical manual of mental disorders (3rd ed.). Washington, DC: American Psychiatric Association.

Ansen, D. (1991, August 12). Paris is burning (review). Newsweek, 118, p. 62

Aptekar, L. (1988). Street children of Cali. Durham, NC: Duke University Press.

Armani or your life. (1992, March 16). U.S. News and World Report, p. 16.

Balshem, M., Oxman, G., van Rooyen, D., & Girod, K. (1992). Syphilis, sex, and crack cocaine: Images of risk and mortality. Social Science Medicine, 35(2), 147-160.

Bannister, D. & Fransella, F. (1971). Inquiring man: The theory of personal constructs. Baltimore: Penguin Books.

Barden, J. (1991, January 6). After release from foster care, many turn to lives on the streets. New York Times, p. 1.

Basie, C. (Composer and Performer) & Martin, S. (Composer). (1991). Miss Thing. *I like jazz: The essence of Count Basie* (Cassette Recording No. 7464-47918-4). New York: Sony Music Entertainment, Inc.

Becker, H. S. (1963). Outsiders: Studies in the sociology of deviance. London: The Free Press of Glencoe, Collier-MacMillian, Ltd., p. 9. Cited in M. Balshem et al. Syphilis, sex, and crack cocaine: Images of risk and mortality. Social Science Medicine, 35(2), 147-160.

Berger, P. & Luckmann, T.C. (1966). The social construction of reality: A treatise in the sociology of knowledge. USA: Anderson Books, pp. 129, 138. Cited in A. Wilkinson (1987). Born to rebel: An ethnography of street kids. Doctoral dissertation, Gonzaga University.

Berger, R.J. (1989). Female delinquency in the emancipation era: A review of the literature. Sex Roles, 21, 375-399.

Bender, L. & Yarnell, H. (1941). An observational nursery. American Journal of Psychiatry, 97, 1158-1174.

Beyer, M. (1974). Psychosocial problems of adolescent runaways. Doctoral dissertation, Yale University.

Bogdan, R. & Taylor, S. (1975). Introduction to qualitative research methods: A phenomenological approach to the social sciences. New York: John Wiley & Sons.

Bogdan, R. & Biklen, S. (1982). Qualitative research for education. Boston: Allyn and Bacon, Inc.

Bollinger, A. (1988a, September 6). Children of the night, Part 1. New York Post, pp. 1, 4-5, 22-23.

Bollinger, A. (1988b, September 7). Children of the night, Part 2. New York Post, pp. 1-3, 18-19.

Bollinger, A. (1988c, September 8). Children of the night, Part 3. New York Post, pp. 2-32, 27.

Bollinger, A. (1988d, September 9). Children of the night, Part 4. New York Post, pp. 4-5, 16.

Bond, L.S., Mazin, R., & Jiminez, M.V. (1992). Street youth and AIDS. AIDS Education and Prevention, Fall Supplement, 14-23.

Bowlby, J. (1966). Maternal care and mental health. New York: Schucken Books.

Boyar, D. (1986). Street exit project. Seattle: U.S. Dept. of Health and Human Services, Office of Human Development Services (Grant 90-C40360).

Brown, M. (1979). Teenage prostitution. Adolescence, 14, 665-680.

Burbridge, R. (1978). The nature and potential of therapeutic humor. Doctoral dissertation, California Institute of Asian Studies.

Calhoun, G., Jurgens, J., & Chen, F. (1993). The neophyte female delinquent: A review of the literature. Adolescence, 28(110), 461-471.

Carlson, V., Cicchetti, D., Barnett, D. & Braunwald, K. (1989). Disorganized/disoriented attachment relationships in maltreated infants. Developmental Psychology, 25, 525-531.

Carini, P. (1975). Observation and description: An alternative methodology for the investigation of human phenomena. Grand Rapids, ND: North Dakota Study Group on Evaluation. n.p. Cited in M. Ely (1984). Beating the odds: An ethnographic interview study of young adults from the culture of poverty. Paper presented at the Seventh Annual Conference on English Education, New York University, New York, p. 6.

Cates, J.A. & Markley, J. (1992). Demographic, clinical, and personality variables associated with male prostitution by choice. Adolescence, 27(107), 695-706.

Caton, C. (1986). The homeless experience in adolescent years. In E. Bassuk (Ed.), The mental health needs of homeless persons (pp. 63-70). San Francisco, CA: Jossey-Bass. New Directions in Mental Health Services, Pub. 30.

Cavaiola, A. & Schiff, M. (1988). Behavioral sequelae of physical and/or sexual abuse in adolescents. Child Abuse and Neglect, 12, 181-188.

Chiauzzi, E.J. (1991). Preventing relapse in the addictions: A biopsychosocial approach. New York: Pergamon Press.

Citizens' Committee for Children of New York. (1983). Homeless youth in New York City: Nowhere to turn. New York: Citizens' Committee for Children of New York Publications.

Clark, C.M. (1992). Deviant adolescent subcultures: Assessment strategies and clinical interventions. Adolescence, 27(106), 283-293.

Cobb, A. & Hagemaster, J. (1987). Ten criteria for evaluating research proposals. Journal of Nursing Education, 26, 138-143.

Covenant House New Jersey. (1990a). AIDS prevention and identification project. Unpublished manuscript.

Covenant House New Jersey. (1990b). Summary of census and service statistics, December 1, 1989 thru July 26, 1990. Unpublished manuscript.

Covenant House New Jersey. (1990c). Summary of client characteristics: End of fiscal year 1990. Unpublished manuscript.

Crespi, T.D. & Sabatelli, R.M. (1993). Adolescent runaways and family strife: A conflict-induced differentiation framework. Adolescence, 28(112), 867-878.

Crittenden, P. M. (1988). Relationships at risk. In J. Belsky and T. Nezworski (Eds.), Clinical implications of attachment. Hillsdale, NJ: Lawrence Erlbaum Associates, Inc., pp. 136-174.

Crystal, S. (1986). Psychosocial rehabilitation and homeless youth. Psychosocial Rehabilitation Journal, 10(2), 15-21.

David, M., & Appell, G. (1961). A study of nursing care and nurse-infant interaction: A report on the first half of an investigation. In B.M. Foss (Ed.). Determinants of infant behavior, (Vol. 1). Methsen, n.p. Cited in M. Rutter (1972). Maternal deprivation reassessed. Baltimore: Penguin Books. (p. 66).

Davies, R. (1977). *Lola. Come Dancing with the Kinks: The Best of the Kinks, 1977-1986*, (Cassette Recording No. AC11-8428). New York: Arista Records and Tapes.

De'Ath, E. & Newman, C. (1987). Children who run. Children and Society, 1(1), 13-18.

Deisher, R. & Farrow, J. (1986). Recognizing and dealing with alienated youth in clinical practice. Pediatric Annals, 15, 759-764.

Deisher, R., Farrow, J. Robinson, G., & Boyar, D. (1982). The adolescent female and male prostitute. Pediatric Annals, 11, 819-825.

Deisher, R.W., Litchfield, C., & Hope, K.R. (1991). Birth outcomes of prostituting adolescents. Journal of Adolescent Health, 12(7), 528-533.

Device and consent. (1992, March 9). U.S. News and World Report, p. 10.

Edwards, B. (Director and Producer). (1982). *Victor/Victoria* [Film]. Hollywood, CA: Metro Goldwyn Myer/United Artists.

Elifson, K.W., Boles, J., Posey, E., Sweat, M., Darrow, W., & Elsea, W. (1993). Male transvestite prostitutes and HIV risk. American Journal of Public Health, 83(2), 260-262.

Ely, M. (1984). Beating the odds: An ethnographic interview study of young adults from the culture of poverty. Paper presented at the Seventh Annual Conference on English Education, New York University, New York.

Ely, M., Anzul, M., Friedman, T., Garner, D. & Steinmetz, A. (1991). Doing qualitative research: Circles within circles. New York: The Falmer Press.

Englander, S. (1984). Some self-reported correlates of runaway behavior in adolescent females. Journal of Consulting and Clinical Psychology, 52, 484-485.

Erikson, E.H. (1982). The life cycle completed. New York: W. W. Norton & Company, Inc.

Ernst, A.A., & Martin, D.H. (1993). High syphilis rates among cocaine abusers identified in an emergency department. Sexually Transmitted Diseases, 20(2), 66-69.

Fagan, J. & Chin, K. (1991). Social processes of initiation into crack. Journal of Drug Issues, 21(2), 313-343.

Farber, E., Kinast, C., McCoard, D. & Falkner, D. (1984). Violence in families of adolescent runaways. Child Abuse & Neglect, 8, 295-299.

Feitel, B., Margetson, N., Chamas, J., & Lipman, C. (1992). Psychosocial background and behavioral and emotional disorders of homeless and runaway youth. Hospital and Community Psychiatry, 43(2), 155-159.

Feuer, C. (Producer) & Fosse, B. (Director). (1972). *Cabaret* [Film]. Hollywood, CA: Feuer & Martin Productions.

Gabriel, T. (1992, January). Bill Evans's twilight zone. Vanity Fair, pp. 58-63.

Garrett, L. (1990, February 6). Hawaii's 'ice'-epidemic babies. New York Newsday, p. 5.

Gelles, R. (1979). Family violence. Beverly Hills, CA: Sage, n.p. Cited in Farber, E., Kinast, C., McCoard, D. & Falkner, D. (1984). Violence in families of adolescent runaways. Child Abuse & Neglect, 8, 295-299.

Goffman, E. (1963). Stigma: Notes on the management of spoiled identity. Englewood Cliffs, NJ: Prentice-Hall, p. 2-3. Cited in M. Balshem, G. Oxman, D. van Rooyen, & K. Girod. Syphilis, sex, and crack cocaine: Images of risk and mortality. Social Science Medicine, 35(2), p. 155.

Golden, S. (1992). The women outside: Meanings and myths of homelessness. Berkeley, CA: University of California Press.

Goldfarb, W. (1943). Infant rearing and problem behavior. American Journal of Orthopsychiatry, 13, pp. 249-265. Cited in Rutter, M. (1972). Maternal deprivation reassessed. Baltimore: Penguin Books.

Goldfarb, W. (1955). Emotional and intellectual consequences of psychological deprivation in infancy: A reevaluation. In P.J. Hock and J. Zubin (Eds.). Psychopathology of childhood. Grune and Stratton, n.p. Cited in M. Rutter (1972). Maternal deprivation reassessed. Baltimore: Penguin Books.

Goldmeier, J. & Dean, R. (1973). The runaway: Person, problem, or situation? Crime and Delinquency, 19, 539-544.

Goldsmith, B. (1993). Women on the edge. The New Yorker, 26 April 1993, 64-81.

Goldstein, P.J., Ouellet, L.J., & Fendrich, M. (1992). From bag brides to skeezers: A historical perspective on drugs-for-sex behavior. Journal of Psychoactive Drugs, 24(4), 349-361.

Green, J. (1993, April 18). Paris has burned: Death is unraveling the world of drag balls depicted in the acclaimed film *Paris is burning*. New York Times, Section 9, pp. 3, 11.

Guba, E. (1981). Criteria for assessing the trustworthiness of naturalistic inquiries. Educational Communication and Technology Journal, 29, 75-91.

Hagan, J. & McCarthy, B. (1992). Streetlife and delinquency. British Journal of Sociology, 43(4), 533-561.

Haley, J. (1973). Uncommon therapy: The psychiatric techniques of Milton H. Erikson, MD. New York: Norton.

Hartman, C., Burgess, A. & McCormack, A. (1987). Pathways and cycles of runaways: A model for understanding repetitive runaway behavior. Hospital and Community Psychiatry, 38, 292-299.

Havighurst, R.J. (1972). Developmental tasks and education (3rd ed.). New York: David McKay Company, Inc, 43-82.

Hersch, P. (1988, January). Coming of age on city streets. Psychology Today, pp. 28, 30-32, 34-37.

Holdaway, D.M., & Ray, J. (1992). Attitudes of street kids toward foster care. Child and Adolescent Social Work Journal, 9(4), 307-317.

Inciardi, J. (1984). Little girls and sex: A glimpse at the world of the "baby pro." Deviant Behavior, 5, 71-78.

Institute of Medicine. (1988). Homelessness, health, and human needs. Washington, DC: Academy Press.

Institute of Medicine. (1989). Research on children & adolescents with mental, behavioral, and developmental disorders (pp. 69-104). Washington, DC: Academy Press.

Inter-NGO. (Program on Street Children and Street Youth). (1983). Document 83/23-SC/35, 18th March. Geneva: International Child and Youth Bureau. Cited in C. Williams, (1993). Who are 'street children?' A hierarchy of street use and appropriate responses. Child Abuse and Neglect, 17(6), 831-841.

Irwin, J. (1970). The felon. Englewood Cliffs, NJ: Prentice-Hall.

Janus, M., Burgess, A. & McCormack, A. (1987). Histories of sexual abuse in adolescent male runaways. Adolescence, 22, 405-417.

Kaplan, L. (1989). Introduction. Children and Youth Services Review, 11, 1-3.

Kelly, G.A. (1955). A theory of personality: The psychology of personal constructs. New York: W. W. Norton & Company, Inc.

Kennedy, J., Petrone, J., Deisher, R., Emerson, J., Heslop, P., Bastible, D. & Arkovitz, M. (1990). Health care for familyless, runaway, street kids. In J. Brickner (Ed.), Under the safety net: The health and social welfare of the homeless in the United States. New York: McMillan & Sons, pp. 82-117.

Kerr, P. (1989, August 20). Crack and resurgence of syphilis spreading AIDS among the poor. The New York Times, pp. 1, 36.

Knaack, P. (1984). Phenomenological research. Western Journal of Nursing Research, 6, 107-114.

Kufeldt, K. & Nimmo, M. (1987). Youth on the street: Abuse and neglect in the eighties. Child Abuse and Neglect, 11, 531-543.

LeBlanc, A.N. (1992, December 8). Trina's story: Three years in the life of a teenage prostitute. The Village Voice, 26-32.

Lecayo, R. (1989, October 9). Nobody's children. Time, p. 92.

Leininger, M. (Ed.) (1985). Qualitative research methods in nursing. Orlando, FL: Grune & Stratton, Inc.

Liebow, E. (1967). Talley's corner: A study of Negro street corner men. Boston: Little, Brown & Co.

Lincoln, Y. & Guba, E. (1985). Naturalistic inquiry. Beverly Hills, CA: Sage.

Lipson, J. (1984). Combining researcher, clinical, and personal roles: Enrichment or confusion? Human Organization, 43, 348-352.

Livingston, J. (Producer and Director). (1990). *Paris is Burning* [Film]. New York: A Jenny Livingston Film.

LoBiondo-Wood, G. & Haber, J. (1990). Nursing research: Methods, critical appraisal, and utilization (2nd ed.). St. Louis: C. V. Mosby Company.

Loeb, R., Burke, T. & Boglarsky, C. (1986). A large-scale comparison of perspectives on parenting between teenage runaways and nonrunaways. Adolescence, 21, 921-30.

Lofland, J. & Lofland, L. (1984). Analyzing social settings: A guide to qualitative observation and analysis (2nd ed.). Belmont, CA: Wadsworth Publishing Company.

Los Angeles County Task Force on Runaway and Homeless Youth. (1988). Report and recommendations of Los Angeles County Task Force on runaway and homeless youth. Los Angeles, CA: Author.

Lothian, J. (1989). Continuing to breastfeed. Doctoral dissertation, New York University.

Luna, G.C. (1991). Street youth: Adaptation and survival in the AIDS decade. Journal of Adolescent Health, 12(7), 511-514.

Manov, A. & Lowther, L. (1983). A health care approach for hard-to-reach adolescent runaways. Nursing Clinics of North America, 18, 333-342.

Martin, M.A. (1982). Strategies of adaptation: Coping patterns of the urban transient female. Doctoral dissertation, Columbia University.

McCall, G., & Simmons, J.L. (Eds.) (1969). Issues in participant observation. Reading, PA: Addison-Wesley, p. 3. Cited in R. Bogdan & S. Taylor (1975). Introduction to qualitative research methods: A phenomenological approach to the social sciences. New York: John Wiley & Sons, p. 5.

McCarthy, B. & Hagan, J. (1992). Surviving on the street: The experiences of homeless youth. Journal of Adolescent Research, 7(4), 412-430.

McGhee, P. (1971). Cognitive development and children's comprehension of humor. Child Development, 42, 123-138.

McMullen, R.J. (1986). Youth prostitution: A balance of power? International Journal of Offender Therapy and Comparative Criminology, 30(3), 237-243.

Miller, A.T., Eggerston-Tacon, C., & Quigg, B. (1990). Patterns of runaway behavior within a larger systems context: The road to empowerment. Adolescence, 25(98), 271-289.

Mirkin, M., Raskin, P. & Antognini, F. (1984). Parenting, protecting, and preserving: Mission of the adolescent female runaway. Family Process, 23, 63-74.

Moore, T.W. (1963). Effects on the children. In S. Yudkin and A. Holme (Eds.). Working mothers and their children. Michael Joseph, n. p. Cited in Rutter, M. (1972). Maternal deprivation reassessed. Baltimore: Penguin Books, p. 101.

Morningstar, P. & Chitwood, D. (1987). How women and men get cocaine: Sex-role sterotypes and acquisition patterns. Journal of Psychoactive Drugs, 19(2), 135-142.

Morse, E., Simon, P., Osofsky, H., Balson, P., & Gaumer, H. (1991). The male street prostitute: A vector for transmission of HIV infection into the heterosexual world. Social Science Medicine, 32(5), 535-539.

Morse, E., Simon, P., Balson, P., & Osofsky, H. (1992). Sexual behavior patterns of customers of male street prostitutes. Archives of Sexual Behavior, 21(4), 347-357.

Moy, J.A., & Sanchez, M.R. The cutaneous manifestations of violence and poverty. Archives of Dermatology, 128(6), 829-839.

Moya, A.E. (1989). La Alfombra de Guazabra o el Reino de los Desterrados. Paper presented at the first Congreso Dominicano Sobre el Menor en Circumstancias Especialmente Dificiles. Santo Domingo, Dominican Republic. Cited in L.S. Bond, R. Mazin, & M.V. Jiminezebe (1992). Street youth and AIDS. AIDS Education and Prevention, Fall Supplement, 14-23.

Murphy, S., & Rosenbaum, M. (1992). Women who use cocaine too much: Smoking crack vs. snorting cocaine. Journal of Psychoactive Drugs, 24(4), 381-388.

Nerlove, S., & Roberts, J. (1975). Natural indicators of cognitive development: An observational study of rural Guatemalan children. ETHOS, 3, pp. 265-295. Cited in L. Aptekar (1988). Street children of Cali. Durham, NC: Duke University Press, p. 31.

Nolan, J. (1990, August 6). On the streets: Crime terrifies West Villagers. New York Post, pp. 3, 13.

Number of AIDS orphans grows (1992). The Post and Courier, 23 December 1992, p. 3a.

Office of the Inspector General. (1983). <u>Runaway and homeless youth: National Program Inspection</u>. Washington, DC: Office of the Inspector General, Department of Health and Human Services, Region X.

Ogbu, S. (1988). Diversity and equity in public education: Community forces and minority school adjustment and performance. In R. Haskin & D. MacRae (Eds.). <u>Policies for Americans public schools: Teachers, equity, and indicators</u>. Norwood, NJ: Ablex Publication Corp., p. 147.

Omery, A. (1983). Phenomenology: A method for nursing research. <u>Advances in Nursing Science</u>. pp. 49-63. Cited in A. Cobb, & J. Hagemaster (1987). Ten criteria for evaluating research proposals. <u>Journal of Nursing Education</u>, <u>26</u>, 138-143.

Opinion Research Corporation. (1976). <u>National statistical survey on runaway youth</u> (Contract No. 105-75-2105). Washington, DC: Department of Health, Education, and Welfare.

Orten, J.D., & Soll, S.K. (1980). Runaway children and their families: A treatment typology. <u>Journal of Family Issues</u>, <u>1</u>(2), 249-261. Cited in A.T. Miller, C. Eggerston-Tacon, & B. Quigg (1990). Patterns of runaway behavior within a larger systems context: The road to empowerment. <u>Adolescence, 25</u>(98), 271-289.

Pagnozzi, A. (1994, May). Killer girls. <u>Elle</u>, 122-126.

Palenski, J. & Launer, H. (1987). The "process" of running away: A redefinition. <u>Adolescence</u>, <u>22</u>, 347-362.

Parent talk: Not so wonderful years. (1991, May 27). <u>The News and Courier</u>, p. D1.

Parse, R., Coyne, A. & Smith, M. (1985). <u>Nursing research: Qualitative methods</u>. Bowie, MA: Brady Communications Company.

Pennbridge, J., MacKenzie, R.G. & Swofford, A. (1991). Risk profile of homeless pregnant adolescents and youth. <u>Journal of Adolescent Health,</u> <u>12</u>(7), 534-538.

Pooley, E. (1990, October 15). The vogue of death. <u>New York,</u> pp. 55-60.

Powers, J.L. & Jaklitsch, B.W. (1989). <u>Understanding survivors of abuse: Stories of homeless and runaway adolescents</u>. Lexington, MA: Lexington Books.

Powers, J., Jaklitsch, B. & Eckenrode, J. (1988, June 15-17). <u>Identifying maltreatment among runaway and homeless youth</u>. Paper presented at the Sixth National Conference on Research, Demonstration and Evaluation in Public Human Services, Washington, DC.

Price, R. (1992). <u>Clockers</u>. New York: Houghton Mifflin.

Price, V. (1989). Characteristics and needs of Boston street youth: One agency's response. <u>Children and Youth Services Review,</u> <u>11</u>, 75-90.

Provence, S. & Lipton, R.C. (1962). Infants in institutions. <u>International Universities Press.</u> n.p. Cited in M. Rutter (1972). <u>Maternal deprivation reassessed</u>. Baltimore: Penguin Books.

Prugh, D. & Harlow, R. (1966). "Masked deprivation" in infants and young children. In J. Bowlby (Ed.), <u>Deprivation of maternal care: A reassessment of its effects</u> New York: Schucken Books, 201-222.

Reed, L. (Composer and Performer). (1989). *Dirty Boulevard.* Lou Reed: New York (Cassette Recording No. 9 25829-4). New York: Sire Records.

Reed, L. (Composer and Performer). (1990). *Walk on the Wild Side. Lou Reed: Walk on the Wild Side & other Hits* (Cassette Recording No. 2162-4-R). New York: BMG Music.

Reinharz, S. (1981). Implementing new paradigm research: A model for training and practice. In P. Reason & J. Rowan (Eds.), Human inquiry New York: J. Wiley & Sons, 415-433.

Reinharz, S. (1983). Experiential analysis: A contribution to feminist research. In C. Bowles & R. Klein (Eds.), Theories of women studies (pp. 162-191). London: Routledge & Kegan Paul.

Rheingold, H.L. (1961). The effects of environmental stimulation upon social and exploratory behaviors in the human infant. In B.M. Foss (Ed.). Determinants of Infant Behavior, p. 1. Cited in Rutter, M. (1972). Maternal deprivation reassessed. Baltimore: Penguin Books.

Rich, O.J. (1990). Maternal-infant bonding in homeless adolescents and their infants. Maternal Child Nursing Journal, 19(3), 195-210.

Ritter, B. (1989). Abuse of the adolescent. New York State Journal of Medicine, 89(3), 156-158.

Roberts, A. (1982a). Stress and coping patterns among adolescent runaways. Journal of Social Service Research, 5, 15-27.

Roberts, A. (1982b). Adolescent runaways in suburbia: A new typology. Adolescence, 17, 387-396.

Robertson, J.M. (1988). Taking issue. Homeless adolescents: A hidden crisis. Hospital and Community Psychiatry, 39, 475.

Robertson, M.J. (1989, April 25-28). Homeless youth: An overview of recent literature. Paper presented at the National Conference on Homeless Children and Youth, Institute for Policy Studies at Johns Hopkins University, Washington, DC.

Rotheram-Borus, M.J. (1993). Suicidal behaviors and risk factors among runaway youths. American Journal of Psychiatry, 150(1), 103-107.

Rotheram-Borus, M.J., Meyer-Bahlburg, H.F.L., Koopman, C., Rosario, M., Exner, T.M., Henderson, R., Matthieu, M., & Gruen, R.S. (1992). Lifetime sexual behaviors among runaway males and females. The Journal of Sex Research, 29(1), 15-29.

Rothman, J. & David, T. (1985). Focus on runaway and homeless youth. Los Angeles: University of California, Bush Program in Social Welfare.

Rutter, M. (1972). Maternal deprivation reassessed. Baltimore: Penguin Books.

Saltonstall, M. (1984). Street youth and runaways on the streets of Boston: One agency's response. Boston: The Bridge, Inc.

Sample, J. (Composer) & Jennings, W. (Composer). (1980). *Street life. Crusaders: Street Life* (Cassette Recording No. 1658). New York: MCA Records.

Sante, L. (1992, July 16). The possessed. The New York Review of Books, pp. 23-25.

Schaffer, B. & DeBlassie, R. (1984). Adolescent prostitution. Adolescence, 19, 689-696.

Schwarcz, S.K., Bolan, G.A., Fullilove, M., McCright, J., Fullilove, R., Kohn, R., & Rolfs, R.T. (1991) Crack cocaine and the exchange of sex for money or drugs. Sexually Transmitted Diseases, 19(1), 7-13.

Sereny, G. (1985). The invisible children: Child prostitution in America, West Germany, and Great Britain. New York: Alfred Knopf.

Shaffer, D. & Caton, C. (1984). Runaway and homeless youth in New York City: A report to the Ittleson Foundation. New York: Ittleson Foundation and New York State Office of Mental Health, Division for Research.

Silbert, M. & Pines, A. (1983). Early sexual exploitation as an influence in prostitution. Social Work, 4, 285-289.

Simon, P.M., Morse, E.V., Osofsky, H.J., Balson, P.M., & Gaumer, H.R. (1992). Psychological characteristics of a sample of male street prostitutes. Archives of Sexual Behavior, 21(1), 33-44.

Skodol, A.E. (1989). Problems in differential diagnosis: From DSM-III to DSM-III-R in clinical practice. Washington, DC: American Psychiatric Press, Inc.

Solotaroff, P. (1990, January 30). Dead boys: Fast sex and slow suicide on the West Side Docks. Village Voice, 33-37.

Speck, N., Ginther, D. & Helton, J. (1988). Runaways: Who will run again? Adolescence, 23, 881-888.

Spillane-Grieco, E. (1984). Characteristics of a helpful relationship: A study of empathic understanding and positive regard between runaways and their parents. Adolescence, 19, 64-75.

Spradley, J. (1979). The ethnographic interview. New York: Holt, Rinehart, and Winston.

Stefanidis, N., Pennbridge, J., MacKenzie, R.G. & Poltharst, K. (1992). Runaway and homeless youth: The effects of attachment history on stabilization. American Journal of Orthopsychiatry, 62(3), 442-446.

Stiffman, A. (1989). Physical and sexual abuse in runaway youths. Child Abuse and Neglect, 13, 417-426.

Streets of sanctuary now harbor criminals. (1990, August 6). The New York Times, pp. B1, B4.

Suggs, D. (1988, May 31). Venus envy: The Harlem Balls take on the world. Village Voice, pp. 23-29.

Sundelin-Wahlsten, V. (1985). The resilient children: The source of health. Psykisk-Hasa, 26(3), 152-154. Abstracted in PsychLIT Disc 2 (1/83-12/91).

Tait, G. (1993). Reassessing street kids: A critique of subculture theory. Child and Youth Care Forum, 22(2), 83-93.

Theis, S. (1924). How foster children turn out. New York: State Charities Aid Assn. n.p. Cited in D. Prugh, & R. Harlow (1966). "Masked deprivation" in infants and young children. In J. Bowlby (Ed.), Deprivation of maternal care: A reassessment of its effects. New York: Schucken Books, 201-222.

Van Sant, G. (Producer and Director). (1991). *My own Private Idaho* [Film]. Portland: New Line Cinema.

Visano, L.A. (1991). The impact of age on paid sexual encounters. Journal of Homosexuality, 20(3-4), 207-226.

Weatherby, N.L., Shultz, J.M., Chitwood, D.D., McCoy, H.V., McCoy, C.B., Ludwig, D.D., & Edlin, B.R. (1992). Crack cocaine use and sexual activity in Miami, Florida. Journal of Psychoactive Drugs, 24(4), 373-380.

Weber, S. (1986). The nature of interviewing. Phenomenology + Pedagogy, 4, 65-72.

Weisberg, D.K. (1985). Children of the night: A study of adolescent prostitution. Lexington MA: Lexington Books.

Werner, E. (1984). Resilient children. Young children, 40, 68-72.

Werner, E. (1989). High-risk children in young adulthood: A longitudinal study from birth to 32 years. American Journal of Orthopsychiatry, 59, 72-81.

Wilkinson, A. (1987). Born to rebel: An ethnography of street kids. Doctoral dissertation, Gonzaga University.

Williams, A. (1977). A comparison study of family dynamics and personality characteristics of runaways and nonrunaways. Doctoral dissertation, United States International University.

Williams, C. (1993). Who are 'street children?' A hierarchy of street use and appropriate responses. Child Abuse and Neglect, 17(6), 8310841.

Williams, T. (1989). Crackhouse: Notes from the end of the line. New York: Addison-Wesley.

Wolk, S. & Brandon, J. (1977). Runaway adolescents' perception of parents and self. Adolescence, 12, 175-187.

Wurzbacher, K.V., Evans, E.D., & Moore, E.J. (1991). Effects of alternative street school on youth involved in prostitution. Journal of Adolescent Health, 12(7), 549-554.

Yancey, A. (1992). Identity formation and social maladaptation in foster adolescents. Adolescence, 27(108), 819-831.

Yates, G., MacKenzie, R., Pennbridge, J. & Cohen, E. (1988). A risk profile comparison of runaway and nonrunaway youth. American Journal of Public Health, 78, 820-821.

Yates, G.L., MacKenzie, R.G., Pennbridge, J., & Swofford, A. (1991). A risk profile of homeless youth involved in prostitution and homeless youth not involved. Journal of Adolescent Health, 12(7), 545-548.

Appendix A

Possible Interview Questions

Tell me your story. How did you get here?

Please tell me about your family. What was it like growing up?

How and when were you introduced to the streets?

How would you describe the streets?

How have you survived out here?

What has it been like for you?

What sort of friendships do you have?

How do you get along with your family now?

What kinds of contacts do you have with helping agencies?

Mainstream society?

Dates? Other street kids?

What is a typical day like for you?

What about drugs and alcohol?

What sort of work have you done? Do you do?

How do you get around? Where might you go?

What would I need to know to survive out here?

Is there anything else you want me to know about life on the streets, or you?

Appendix B

Explanation of the Study
To Participants

My purpose in this study is to gain information about the daily living experience of kids on the streets from their point of view. Your participation may be either through observation by and conversation with the researcher and one or two interviews lasting one to one and a half hours each.

Your participation is voluntary and you have the right to withdraw from the study at any time. You will not be identified by name or other identifying characteristics in the research material or resulting publications or presentations.

The principle investigator of this study is Katherine Lundy, M.S.N., R.N., doctoral candidate. This research is being conducted under the supervision of John Phillips, Ph.D., R.N., in partial fulfillment of the requirements for the degree of Doctor of Philosophy from the Program in Research and Theory Development in Nursing Science at New York University. The investigator will be available to answer any questions regarding this study at 803 577-0819.

Thank you for your cooperation.

Katherine Coleman Lundy

Appendix C

Consent Form

I agree to participate in the Study of Street Kids which is a partial requirement for the Degree of Ph.D. in Nursing at New York University. I understand that:

My purpose in this research is to obtain a better understanding of what life is like for street kids from their point of view. Findings from this study may be useful in the later development of nursing practice, research, and education.

All responses will be treated confidentially. My name will not be used in any written report or publication of the study or findings.

Participation in the study will involve either direct observation and conversation with the researcher in a public area or one or two personal interviews with the researcher. The interviews will be tape-recorded and each will require one to one and a half hours of my time.

Contents of the tape belong to me and I may request them or ask that they be destroyed. I understand that tapes will be kept in a protected location and erased at the conclusion of the research.

Results of this study will be published and presented to the scientific community for use in further development of scientific knowledge in nursing and other disciplines. I may request a summary of the study from the researcher.

I have received a copy of this form to keep. I have the right to ask questions about the study or to refuse to participate or to withdraw at any time without jeopardy.

If I have any questions about the study, I may contact the researcher at the address and telephone number below.

Katherine Coleman Lundy   Name _____
PO Box 20811   (please print)
Charleston, SC 29413
803 577-0819   Address _____

Signature _____

Index